RAISING LILLY LEDBETTER
Women Poets Occupy the Workspace

RAISING LILLY LEDBETTER
Women Poets Occupy the Workspace

Edited by

Carolyne Wright

M. L. Lyons

& Eugenia Toledo

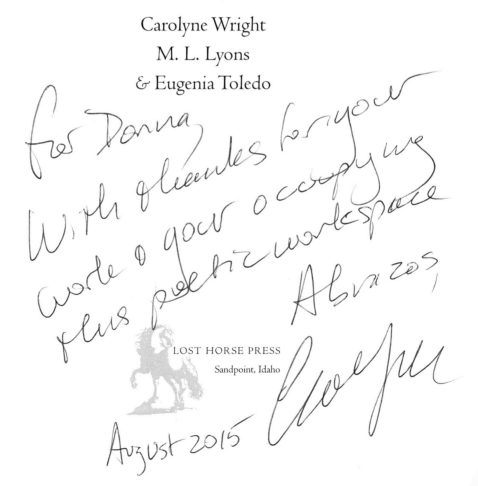

For Donna,
With greetings for your
work & your occupying
plus poetic workspace

Abrazos,

August 2015

LOST HORSE PRESS
Sandpoint, Idaho

The editors and publisher of this anthology extend our gratitude to the BONNER COUNTY ENDOWMENT FUND FOR HUMAN RIGHTS IN THE IDAHO COMMUNITY FOUNDATION for their generous grant that has significantly supported our campaign to recognize, honor, and champion working women everywhere.

Cover Art: Lilly Ledbetter photo used by permission of REUTERS/Jessica Rinaldi.
Book & Cover Design: Christine Holbert

FIRST EDITION

This and other LOST HORSE PRESS titles may be viewed online at *www.losthorsepress.org.*

LIBRARY OF CONGRESS CATALOGING-IN-PUBLICATION DATA
Raising Lilly Ledbetter : women poets occupy the workspace / edited by Carolyne Wright, M. L. Lyons & Eugenia Toledo.—First edition.
     pages cm
Includes bibliographical references.
ISBN 978-0-9911465-9-8 (alk. paper)
1. Poetry—Women authors. 2. Women employees—Poetry. 3. Work—Poetry. I. Wright, Carolyne, 1949-editor. II. Lyons, M. L., editor. III. Toledo, Eugenia, editor.
PN6109.9.R35 2015
809.1'99287—dc23
                    2014050222

In memory and in honor of
Carolyn Kizer (1924 -2014),
to whose poetic Union of Women we all belong.

TABLE OF CONTENTS

IV   CORPORATE IDENTITIES

A STATEMENT BY LILLY LEDBETTER

IN 1979, I WENT TO WORK as a supervisor at a Goodyear tire plant in Gadsden, Alabama. Toward the end of my career, I began to suspect that I wasn't getting paid as much as men doing similar jobs. Of course, it was hard to be sure, because pay levels were a big secret. But an anonymous person left a piece of paper in my mailbox at work one day, comparing my pay with what three male managers were getting paid.

And that's when I knew I'd been the victim of pay discrimination—for a few decades. It turned out that I was earning seventy to seventy-five percent of what my male colleagues were getting. I started at the same salary, but they gave me lower raises—over and over and over again. As you can imagine, over the years those differences added up.

I thought about just moving on, but in the end, I could not let Goodyear get away with it. That turned out to be a life-changing decision for me. If you'd told me then that I'd end up in the Supreme Court, and that Congress would pass a law with my name on it, I'd have said that somebody had let the air out of one of your tires. But that's the path I started down when I brought my lawsuit.

At trial, the jury agreed with me that Goodyear had broken the law, and they awarded me $3 million in back pay, and for mental anguish and punitive damages. That was enough, I hoped, that Goodyear would feel the sting and learn the lesson. The trial judge reduced the award to $300,000, because of a statutory cap on civil rights damages. Don't ask me what that is. All I know is that it made their discrimination a lot less pricey, and less painful, for Goodyear.

But then the Supreme Court, by one vote, took that away, too, saying that I should have filed my complaint within six months of the original act of discrimination, even though I had no way of knowing about it, let alone having enough evidence to complain, at the time. Justice Ruth Bader Ginsburg was not pleased. In her dissent, she wrote that the Court majority's ruling made no sense in the real world. You can't expect people to go around asking their coworkers how much money they're making. And even if you knew that some people were getting paid a little more than you were, that's not a reason to suspect discrimination right away.

So when all was said and done in the courts, there were a few harsh realities. I worked hard at Goodyear, and I was good at my job. But for years and years, with every paycheck I received, I got less than I should have earned, less than I deserved, and less than I was entitled to under the law. But because Goodyear succeeded in keeping this discrimination a secret, five Justices of the Supreme Court of the United States said it didn't matter.

Let me tell you, it matters to me. And it doesn't feel any less like discrimination because it started a long time ago. Quite the opposite, in fact. With each smaller paycheck, Goodyear just piled insult upon insult and injury upon injury. And to this day, the discrimination persists. My pension and Social Security are based on the amount I earned while working there. So the company gets to keep my extra pension money as a reward for breaking the law and covering it up long enough to satisfy a narrow majority on the Supreme Court.

My court case is over now. I may have lost the battle, but I won the war. Goodyear will never have to pay me what it cheated me out of, but with the Lilly Ledbetter Fair Pay Act, I have an even richer reward because I know that my daughters and granddaughters, daughters and granddaughters everywhere, will be fairly compensated for their work. My goal in life now is to continue the work for women to gain true equality in pay, benefits, promotions, power and respect. There is still a lot of work to be done for women to have true equality, so I am happy to know of this collection of poems by women who have carried on the same kinds of struggles as I have. I wish the editors great success with this, and hope it will help to move readers and workers to continue the struggle.

—Lilly Ledbetter, *February 2015*

SEVENTY-SEVEN CENTS TO THE DOLLAR:
A WORKING INTRODUCTION

THE STORY OF LILLY LEDBETTER'S STRUGGLE for justice was the catalyzing force for this anthology, a story representative of the work experiences of millions of women. The first legislation that President Barack Obama signed into law after taking office in January 2009 was the Lilly Ledbetter Fair Pay Act, which restored protections against pay discrimination that had been stripped away by the Supreme Court's decision in Ledbetter v. Goodyear Tire & Rubber Co. In her original lawsuit, Lilly Ledbetter—who had worked for Goodyear as an area manager (a post held almost entirely by men) for nearly two decades—charged that her long-time employer had for years been paying her significantly less than male counterparts with the same job title and similar responsibilities. The higher she rose in rank and responsibility, the greater the discrepancy between her pay and that of her male colleagues, including many with less education, less training, and fewer years on the job.

Although Ledbetter had the evidence to prove the long-term pay discrimination, the Supreme Court struck down her case on a technicality: she had not filed suit within 180 days of the *first instance* of wage inequity—that is, the first unequal paycheck from years before—and thus the statute of limitations to file suit had run out long ago. This was a maddening Catch-22, since Ledbetter had no way to know about the inequity at the time it started, or any time thereafter. Information about fellow employees' pay was confidential at Goodyear, as it continues to be at most workplaces. Sharing information about pay has been a nearly universal, long-standing taboo among American workers—in many companies, it is even a firing offense. In fact, Ledbetter, who had started working at Goodyear in 1979, learned of her own longstanding pay inequity only because a coworker anonymously slipped payroll documents into her mailbox shortly before her early retirement in 1998.

Ledbetter filed a complaint with the Equal Employment Opportunity Commission, her case went to trial, and the jury awarded her back pay and several million dollars in compensatory and punitive damages for the discrimination she had suffered. But Goodyear appealed, and the Eleventh Circuit's Court of Appeals reversed the jury verdict, holding that the case was filed too late, long after the 180-day statute of limitation had expired. Ledbetter took her suit to the Supreme Court where, in May 2007, in a 5-4 decision handed down by Justice Samuel Alito, the Supreme Court upheld the Eleventh Circuit's decision. This ruling upset longstanding precedent under Title VII of the Civil Rights

Act of 1964, stripped away protections of the first Equal Pay Act of 1963, and undermined the widely supported goal of eliminating discrimination in the workplace.

In the spirited dissent that she wrote and uncharacteristically read aloud from the bench, Justice Ruth Bader Ginsburg argued against applying the 180-day limit to pay discrimination, because such discrimination often occurs in small increments over long periods of time. Furthermore, the employer was "knowingly carrying past pay discrimination forward" from one 180-day increment to the next, thus reinstating the same discriminatory action over and over, and creating incentives for employers to continue such discrimination indefinitely—and to benefit from it. She also proclaimed, with word play probably intended, that once again the ball (to reinstate legal protections against pay inequities) was "in Congress' court."

Congress acted quickly in response. After President Obama's election, both the House and Senate passed the Lilly Ledbetter Fair Pay Act of 2009, which reinstated the longstanding protections of prior law and helped to ensure that individuals subjected to unlawful pay discrimination are able to assert their rights under federal law. Under the Act, each discriminatory paycheck, not just the original check reflecting a decision to discriminate, would reset the 180-day limit to file a claim. Moreover, the law was made retroactive to May 28, 2007, the day before the Supreme Court's ruling in Ledbetter v. Goodyear. The Act did not, however, restore Lilly Ledbetter's own lost wages and benefits from two decades of employment discrimination, or the damages originally awarded to her as a result of the jury trial, but it re-invigorated a major national conversation.

Lilly Ledbetter's story resonated with many women in this country—in countless workplaces, by women in all fields of endeavor. As I followed her case during the presidential campaign and through the economic crisis of 2008, I found myself talking with women friends and fellow poets about work. Not just about unequal pay, but all aspects of our working lives: how poets in particular choose careers and support themselves has been of keen interest to me throughout my working life. What sorts of employment we hold, and how much time we spend at work—toiling at jobs we hate or merely endure, or jobs we are lucky enough to love—in order to feed and clothe and house ourselves, and carve out time for writing. Then, as the economic crisis led to large-scale layoffs, how much time the newly unemployed among us had to spend looking for work! At least a third of our waking lives is taken up with work—yet how little poets seemed to write about this essential effort of economic survival and (if we are fortunate to have fulfilling employment) professional expression. Along with our families, the jobs we hold give shape, texture, context, and a schedule around which we build the rest of our lives, yet we don't write much about them! Or do we? That is what the editors of this anthology set out to explore.

On 29 January 2009, when President Obama signed the Lilly Ledbetter Fair Pay Act into law, I began to think about the need to hear more from women about the workspaces they occupy—not just about pay and promotion inequity, or workplace harassment and intimidation, but all matters relevant to women in an increasingly globalized work environment, including the ever more diverse range of jobs and occupations in which women are now engaged, and their joy and satisfaction of work well done. I wondered what poets (the "unacknowledged legislators of the world" as Percy Shelley famously proclaimed in "A Defence of Poetry")—in this case, women poets—were thinking and experiencing in their working lives. A few weeks after the President signed the Lilly Ledbetter Act, I was riding AMTRAK back from the annual conference of the Association of Writers and Writing Programs (AWP), held in Chicago that year, talking with Lost Horse Press' intrepid Founding Editor, Christine Holbert, who had published a book of mine a few years before. Before Christine de-trained in north Idaho, we began talking about her efforts for the Bonner County Human Rights Task Force, on whose board of directors she served. The train glided under a night sky heavy with winter clouds, and we gazed out at snow- and alpine-fir covered slopes as Christine described the Human Rights Series of anthologies that she was planning to support with publication by Lost Horse Press. As the wheels groaned on their steel tracks along curves following the course of the Kootenai River and down to Lake Pend Oreille into Sandpoint, Christine asked me what project I might have in mind for this series. I began telling her my idea for an anthology about women and work—women poets responding in some way to Lilly Ledbetter and her struggle for justice, with poems about our experiences in the workplace. "Somehow," I mused, "such an anthology ought to try to raise Lilly Ledbetter as an issue, because what happened to her is representative of our own concerns as women and as poets who work for a living!" With that, the seed for *Raising Lilly Ledbetter* was planted.

Christine got off the train in Sandpoint, I rode on to Seattle, and a few more years passed, taken up by book projects already underway with Lost Horse and other publishers. But as the 2012 presidential campaign got underway— with debates about layoffs, high unemployment, home foreclosures on a massive scale, the controversial but job-saving rescue of the auto industry, the Occupy Movement's protest encampments in lower Manhattan and elsewhere that focused public attention on vast income inequalities and the role of Wall

Street in creating the economic collapse that caused the greatest recession in generations—Christine and I decided that the time had come for *Raising Lilly Ledbetter*. This anthology would occupy my workspace for the next three years—and also give the book its subtitle. First with Seattle-based Chilean poet Eugenia Toledo (with whom I had collaborated on reciprocal translation projects and a Partners of the Americas-sponsored return trip to Chile in late 2008); and later with poet and editor M. L. Lyons, I set out to edit an anthology of poetry by and about women in the workplace, knowing that it would be a daunting, yet important task. We hoped to bring together voices of women poets in their workspaces—from cotton rows to corner suites, trawlers to typing pools, nursing stations to space stations, factory floors to faculty offices. We sought to discover and highlight the experiences of these women workers, much as Studs Terkel illuminated the lives of working people in his interviews; as Woody Guthrie celebrated workers in song; and as the iconic Mary Harris—"Mother" Jones (at one time called "the most dangerous woman in America")—fought for the working class in labor strikes, union organizing, and a seminal autobiography. Hovering in the back of our minds was the famous image of Rosie the Riveter from World War II—her sleeve rolled up, bicep flexed and fist clenched, and the motto above her head: "We Can Do It!" Rosie was an emblem for us of women's power to take on "a man's job" in shipyards and munitions factories during the war effort, to grow in self-confidence and economic clout, and to continue working when the war ended and the men came home—that is, a symbol for social change that laid the foundation for the woman's movement, and the growing number of workspaces that women occupy today.

The issue of women in the workspace had personal resonance for us editors as well. My child-self moved in the ambience of my brilliant mother's keen sense of injustice, and I listened to her stories of working as the personal secretary for the director of a company—today her position would be called Office Manager. When I was in high school and beginning to contemplate careers, she would recount how, at her last job (which she had quit a decade earlier) she had handled all the company's correspondence and record-keeping, including payroll. So she knew that the new hires whom she trained—all young men—were paid *starting* salaries higher than what she received after all her experience, all her responsibilities, all her years with the company. "Because I'm a woman," she would mutter, shuddering with rage and glancing away. "The unfairness of it just burns me up." Like many women of her generation—born just before the Great War, graduating high school a year after the Stock Market Crash, starting college on a New York State Regent's scholarship but then dropping out to do office work throughout the Depression and the next war, marrying my father and moving West with him when that war ended, giving birth to three children—my mother had ambitions for a career that would employ her intellect, her research and writing skills, but her dreams were never realized.

My mother encouraged my creative and career interests, though, and urged me not to pass up any opportunities. "Say yes to everything!" she would declare with a chuckle: "within reason, of course!" Prospects for her daughter's future were among the few things that brought a smile to her face. And I was keen to pursue a life that she could not have experienced—this spirit of adventure led me from graduate school to writing fellowships in this country and abroad: first Chile and Brazil, then India, then Bangladesh. The fellowships in Kolkata and Dhaka extended during years when I might have been landing and locking into a tenure-track creative writing position back in the U.S., as most others in my cohort of poets did. But at the time, I was not yet ready to stay in one place, and by the time I returned to the U.S., ready to "settle down" in an ongoing position, all of my job searches concluded with offers of full-time visiting posts. Most of these carried some prestige because of the extensive publications required of applicants, and most provided decent salaries and benefits but no prospects of a longer appointment. For over a dozen years I moved from job to job, state to state, with my entire small household of books and manuscripts, clothes and household items, and no fixed address. One reviewer called me the "scholar gipsy" of my generation, with displacement as my permanent address . . . until I arrived with a visiting post in Ohio, where I met the man who would become my husband, moved to Cleveland to join him, taught for one more visiting year at Cleveland State, and then moved with him to my native Seattle. Here I have held the same position in a low-residency MFA program for nearly ten years—here I am paid a modest salary supplemented by other modest "income streams" from freelance editing, short-term teaching posts, and fellowships. But this is a fulfilling life, with a home base in my home town, and blessed both with flexibility for professional travel and an external stability that mirrors—at last!—the internal stability that was essential to staying balanced over so many years of job odyssey.

But such a "working writer's" life has depended on my spouse's holding a "real" job that provided the majority of income and all of the benefits—a common circumstance for many women (and some men) who write. Those years as a "permanent temporary" have marked me, though, and I have found myself gravitating to employment issues in the news, in the lives of friends, and in the national and international sphere. Hence this anthology.

Eugenia Toledo's life has involved major, wrenching displacements. Daughter of a homemaker and a metallurgist who ran a foundry that produced specialized parts for industrial machinery, Eugenia grew up in the southern Chilean city of Temuco, in the same neighborhood as had Pablo Neruda several decades earlier. Her advanced studies in Philology (linguistics) at the Austral University of Valdivia and her career teaching literature at the Catholic University in Temuco were well underway when the U.S.-backed military coup of September 11, 1973, overthrew the democratically elected President Salvador Allende, who died along with thousands of his associates and sent into exile many supporters, including friends of Eugenia's. In the terror and chaos after the coup, Chilean universities remained closed indefinitely by military decree, and Eugenia's instructorship was suspended—because, she believes, authorities at the Catholic University did not like her points of view or her teaching requests at a time of uncertainty for the future of the Arts and Humanities in the country. With academic career prospects in her native country effectively terminated, Eugenia applied for graduate studies in the U.S., and came to Seattle in 1975 to complete masters and doctoral degrees in Latin American Literature at the University of Washington. But after marriage to an American, and the 1986 birth of her son, she didn't have the option to move anywhere she might be offered a university teaching position, so Eugenia stayed in Seattle and taught Spanish in public and private schools, as a low-paid instructional assistant, while her husband traveled world-wide for his job. In 2001, the year of the second 9-11, Eugenia resumed writing again, studying, teaching workshops, and publishing on her own as an independent writer.

M. L. (Mary) Lyons also dealt with her share of political and cultural upheavals, both in her family history and during her childhood growing up in the U.S. Lyons' father was a political refugee who fled Iran following the American and British oil company-backed overthrow of Iran's first democratically elected prime minister, Mohammad Mossadegh, during the 1950s. Lyons' father, Ali Asghar Vahabzadeh, had been a supporter of Mossadegh, and had been imprisoned and tortured in the infamous Evin prison in Tehran for three years following the CIA-sponsored coup. Upon his release from prison, Vahabzadeh fled to the U.S. and began a new life as an economics professor in Southern California, with a non-Persian name and identity, so as to go unnoticed in his adopted country and protect his family's safety. Mary was born in Los Angeles and grew up in a blended Persian-American family with a rich tradition of Persian poetry and literature. As a result of her father's immigrant perspective, she was raised with a dual awareness of life as a Persian-American. Trained in Farsi, she wrote her MFA thesis based on her own translations of the poetry of Forugh Farrokhazad. With an MA degree as well in Publishing, Mary has worked as a publicist and screenwriter in the entertainment industry, as a college instructor, as a marketing communications writer for IT firms, and as an editor and grant-writer for literary arts organizations in the Northwest. The heightened awareness of all three editors, each from her own perspective, of the uncertainties and vicissitudes of the world of work—for everyone but particularly for women—have helped us focus on the issues explored in this anthology!

Our call for submissions to *Raising Lilly Ledbetter*—in *Poets & Writers*, on social media sites and via networks such as *VIDA: Women in Literary Arts*—went out to "women poets of all backgrounds who have occupied spaces in the work force." Eugenia and I asked prospective contributors, "How can women tell their workplace stories in poetry, and be agents of change, locally and globally, particularly in these difficult economic times?" Later, Mary brought another question to the editorial mix: "How do we acknowledge, and dignify, the work that women must do for a living, when these same women might also want other more meaningful work that is paid better and accorded greater social status?" We were heartened and inspired by the breadth of response of poets from all walks of life and work, whose recounting of and reflections upon their working lives moved and impacted us. We heard not just from those who identify primarily and publish widely as poets, but from practitioners of other professions—such as physicist and Professor of Physics Stacey K. Vargas, and her friend and colleague, Professor of Spanish and Women's and Gender Studies, Ellen Mayock. In an email message to me, Vargas wrote that she and Mayock "started [their] creative works as therapy to recover" from their own struggles with workplace discrimination, "but now we are using them as ways to raise awareness and help others to free themselves." We applauded the courage and urgency with which all these poets, experienced and emerging alike, shared their work with us.

We received submissions in hard copy at first—with these, Eugenia and I could meet at a favorite coffee shop in downtown Seattle's "financial district," spread the packets out over the table, read and discuss each group of poems, and then provisionally rate them. After Eugenia needed to return to Chile for an extended period in the wake of her father's death, I was introduced to M. L. (Mary) Lyons at an organizational meeting for another literary project, and she soon joined me in the Lilly Ledbetter endeavor, rendering invaluable editorial assistance. While reading all the submissions and giving her feedback, Mary took on many practical tasks—sending out acceptance (and rejection) messages, researching contacts and background information, preparing an ever-expanding spread sheet of contributors' information and accepted poems; and toward the end of our editorial process, proposing an order for the poems, including sections and section titles, that conferred an implicit narrative arc upon the work. This proposed order created an armature upon which to form the anthology's final shape.

One of the hardest tasks was to make definitive selections. As we might have guessed, there was a wealth of material from which to choose about so-called "women's work": waitressing, secretarial, nursing, domestic labor, teaching at all levels, with the teaching of writing not surprisingly the most common pedagogical expression for poets. Less common were poems from and about women in the sciences; the military, law and government; the higher echelons of business and corporate life. We were pleased with the quality of these, however, and also with the number of fine poems we received about accomplished historical figures in the sciences—Madame Curie, Caroline Herschel (astronomer), Maria Mitchell (mathematician and astronomer), and Augusta Ada Byron King, Countess of Lovelace, Lord Byron's daughter (mathematician) among them. Some of these are persona poems, as are some of the historical figures in the arts—Artemisia Gentileschi (Italian baroque painter), Camille Claudel (French sculptor and assistant to Rodin), Dorothy Dandridge (mid-20th century African-American actress, singer and dancer), and Macuilxochitzin (legendary court poet for the last Aztec rulers of Mexico). There were figures of heroic generosity here—including Osceola McCarty, the Mississippi washerwoman who never finished school but donated $150,000, her lifetime savings, to the University of Southern Mississippi for a scholarship for needy students. We were also heartened by the number of poems of women employed outdoors—ranching, commercial fishing, laboring on construction sites and park trail maintenance crews, gathering traditional foods. Women in the skilled trades were well-represented, as were women in manufacturing—factories! Our quirky favorite work site, of course, was the dildo factory!

The "oldest profession" made its appearance as well—in nuanced tones: no poems on the violence of sex trafficking, none on the crime of child porn, though we would have welcomed such to consider. Instead, we heard from strong women in difficult circumstances, dealing with dire economic conditions; and the voices of ironic but forceful push-back to society's shaming and blaming of sex workers who deal with the erotic dependency of the so-called "stronger sex." In fact, we were gratified at the range of tonalities in these women's voices across all the workspaces—there was some outrage, of course, at workplace inequities, but also lyricism, nostalgia, expressions of pleasure and professional confidence, companionship with other women and with supportive male friends and family members, full-bodied affirmations and energetic humor. There are no "man-hating" rants or angry screeds against the economic order here—we didn't even receive such submissions! We have chosen work that surprised and delighted us with its strength and rigor as poetry, its subtlety and nuance, its wit and elegance, its passion and clarity of thought and image. We are also gratified by the demographic diversity of voices represented here: women of color, Native women, women of immigrant backgrounds; nationally renowned as well as emerging poets.

We initially hoped for a more international scope, but given practical considerations like weight and the cost of shipping overseas, as well as the title's allusion to a U.S. legislative act, we reluctantly determined, with some exceptions (including a number of Canadian poets) to focus on poets of this country. In light of the anthology's core issue of fair pay for work, the poets included here have acted with great generosity to contribute their poems to this non-profit enterprise, their only honorarium a contributor's copy. Only one poet declined to be included because of the lack of honorarium. With the swelling size of the volume, we decided early on to feature only one poem per poet, which occasioned a few difficult choices: Jan Beatty's waitress giving hard-hitting advice about tipping; or her bold, wild-haired bank teller talking back to impatient customers as she helps one gentleman with a complex transaction? (We had a few powerful waitresses already, and no other bank tellers.) Penelope Scambly Schott's poem set in a genteel "Madame's" parlor in pioneer-era Portland, Oregon; or her first-job experience of making donuts for Scrumpy's Cider Mill? (The upscale red-light district parlor was unique in its ironic treatment of the "clientele," and thus prevailed over fast-food preparation.) Should we choose Luisa A. Igloria's scathing critique of discrimination against Filipino immigrants trying to create a better life in their new country? Or her "Ten Thousand Villages," which confronts the complex relationship between craftswomen in developing countries and their first-world female customers, as first-world tastes influence the goods produced—a marketplace that both provides livelihood and a degree of independence for poor women, and simultaneously recapitulates some features of colonialist determinism. ("Ten Thousand Villages" won out—for its more direct treatment of work by women.)

Nonetheless, we were sorry to decline the work of many poets writing about a range of occupations, particularly those who submitted poems about teaching—by far the profession most heavily represented in submissions. As we read incoming material, we realized that we needed to balance representation of the widest possible range of occupations with inclusion of what in our estimation was the best work. Hence, we had a sort of "buyer's market" for poems about teaching and a few of the other most commonly portrayed occupations employing women. Given the urgency and timeliness of our subject matter, and our desire to present work that was both rigorous and accessible to a wide readership, we tended to favor poems that embodied Pound's first two tenets of Imagism: "Direct treatment of the 'thing,' whether subjective or objective"; and "To use absolutely no word that does not contribute to the presentation." Poems, that is, whose specificity of detail, vivid imagery and linguistic compression lent power to their diction . . . and permitted us to fit a few more of these poems within our page limit!

As we received and responded to submissions for *Raising Lilly Ledbetter*, it became clear that work and workers were in the literary Zeitgeist. Did our calls for submissions create ripples and eddies in the currents of poetry? Was it coincidental that the University of Utah's literary magazine, *Western Humanities Review*, published an issue in 2012 on work? Christine forwarded emails to me from the managing editor of this issue, with the exclamation-marked note, "It's in the air, C!" Then the 2014 issue of Seattle-based independent journal, *Floating Bridge Review*, featured a special section, guest-edited by Washington State Poet Laureate Elizabeth Austen, called "Help Wanted: the Poetry of Work." We were pleased to receive copies of these magazines, and to experience their approach to concerns similar to our own: the "inner life of work," as Austen calls it in her introduction, the "place (both literal and metaphorical) where we spend the bulk of our waking hours." Although work, Austen declares, "is not something we get many opportunities to contemplate," the feature she has curated offers a number of perspectives surrounding employment and poets' mixed feelings toward it. These wide-ranging periodical offerings have served to anticipate the more comprehensive, but more specifically focused representation of women's perspectives on work in *Raising Lilly Ledbetter*.

Whereas Austen's vision was for "what is hidden beneath the *doing*," we have been intrigued with the doing itself: the direct treatment of the actions of work, and how those actions influence and shape the internal and external lives of the women performing these jobs—how the tedium, terror, and temptations of the workspace have called forth the voices of women in the poems presented here. This anthology deals with work from the perspective of all that is "Not on Our Resumes." Many of the jobs—early as well as ongoing—of our contributors have given their writing an edge and a political sharpness because, even if they are now employed in better-paid, higher status occupations, they can understand from experience the non-privileged working of many women. And we hope that this anthology will not only extend the conversation, but spark future discussions from and about those who occupy workspaces of all kinds.

Six years after the signing of the Lilly Ledbetter Fair Pay Act, women's average pay in the U. S. has inched up from 77 cents for every dollar earned by men, to a whopping 77.4 cents! Pay for women of color has continued to average even lower. Despite the activism of the Occupy Movement, attempts at more congressional legislation, and a rising minimum wage in many states, women's overall pay continues to lag, except at the highest levels of elite careers, where most of us will never work! During the slowest economic recovery in generations, two-thirds of American families depend fully or in part upon women's paychecks. Clearly, the issue of equal pay for equal work has not gone away. The Lilly Ledbetter Fair Pay Act is significant for women of the present and future—if it can be enforced and its loopholes closed. The economic crisis of 2008, followed by years of recession, stagnant and even dropping wages, part-time jobs supplanting full-time work and benefits, and a recovery that benefits relatively few—all these factors threaten to undermine the gains for women that the Lilly Ledbetter Act promises. Thus, over the years of painstaking and gratifying work on this anthology, the issues it touches on continue to resonate with as much urgency as ever.

THIS BOOK WOULD NOT HAVE BEEN POSSIBLE without the advice, practical assistance and persistence of a small workforce of women (and at least one gent). Lilly Ledbetter herself served as our initial inspiration in her example of women's struggles for workplace fairness—she has been, as it were, our senior colleague and office mentor. The collaboration of Eugenia Toledo and M.L. Lyons, my detail-oriented team players—also known as co-editors—is evident throughout this volume. I am grateful for their insights, friendship, and dedicated labor. Some contributors (and one poet not represented here) suggested names and contact information for other poets who have written about work—these contacts led to a number of key poetic contributions to this book: thank you, Martha Collins, Susan Eisenberg, Melissa Kwasny, Dorianne Laux, Allison Joseph, and Lenard D. Moore. Immense gratitude goes to my husband and partner in rhyme, Jim Parrott, for his incisive editorial suggestions, relentless encouragement, and the patience of a brace of Jobs. And thanks above all to Christine Holbert—daughter of Ukrainian freedom fighters; fierce and fearless Founding Editor, Publisher, and Book Designer Extraordinaire of Lost Horse Press—who first invited this anthology and who has supported it, and us, throughout our labors in bringing it to completion.

—*Carolyne Wright*

Carolyn Kizer

UNION OF WOMEN

At a literary gathering in Santa Monica
I encounter a bearded lady wearing a union button.
We engage each other in friendly conversation:
When I was a little girl in Spokane, Washington,
I took enormous satisfaction in the label
Sewn to my clothes by the Ladies Garment Workers Union.
I was contributing to the Wealth of Women
As I chose my dresses. O Solidarity! O Feminism!
Much later I met a Ladies Garment Workers Union
Leader who told me that she was the only woman
Who'd ever been an official in that union,
Always ignored, outvoted. I felt retrospectively cheated.
Now my new friend, the one with the white beard (she
Won't mind if I mention it, she wrote a cinquain about it)
Says that her Local 814 (mostly women) engages in struggle
With the terrible Sheraton, its unfair labor practices
Concerning the ladies who change the beds and mop the bathrooms,
And fold the ends of the toilet paper
Into those stupid triangles, and put the mints on the pillow.
Of course they're all blacks (I mean African Americans)
Or Mexicans who hardly speak English and fear deportation.
It's clear my bearded friend though old and lame is a fighter;
And she writes excellent cinquains: she just sent me a bunch.
(You know what a cinquain is? A nifty form in five lines
Adapted by Crapsey from the medieval French.)
She, as the current jargon has it, made my day.
So here's to Solidarity, cinquains, brave bearded ladies—Hooray!

I

ENTERING THE WORKFORCE

Rita Dove

MY MOTHER ENTERS THE WORK FORCE

The path to ABC Business School
was paid for by a lucky sign:
Alterations, Qualified Seamstress Inquire Within.
Tested on sleeves, hers
never puckered—puffed or sleek,
leg o'mutton or raglan—
they barely needed the damp cloth
to steam them perfect.

Those were the afternoons. Evenings
she took in piecework, the treadle machine
with its locomotive whir
traveling the lit path of the needle
through quicksand taffeta
or velvet deep as a forest.
And now and now sang the treadle,
I know, I know. . . .

And then it was day again, all morning
at the office machines, their clack and chatter
another journey—rougher,
that would go on forever
until she could break a hundred words
with no errors—ah, and then

no more postponed groceries,
and that blue pair of shoes!

Elayne Clift

WOMEN'S WORK, CIRCA 1943

Laughter was good. Lunchtime was good.
Laboring to build ships, bit by bit, was good.
Friendship was golden. Freedom was grand.
Friday paychecks, and parties, were swell.
They were a sisterhood then, a bevy of
beauties in their drab overalls
and flowered babushkas.
They had tasted the sweetness of self
and savored its deep, silent pleasure.
When it was over, they separated,
returning, subdued, to their secret,
isolated lives, and longed—
not for war, but for just a little bit more.

Andrena Zawinski

ROSIE TIMES

> "How do you know you are going to die?"
> I begged my mother . . . With strange confidence she answered,
> "When you can no longer make a fist."
>
> *—Naomi Shihab Nye*

My mother, born into the flapper era, never bobbed
her hair, never sported drop waist dresses with a cloche,
nor did she cover her face with pancake and rouge,
lifting her skirt above her knees in speakeasies
or on Gatsby verandas. She came of age in World War II.
Draped in white coveralls, hair wrapped in a red scarf
under a hardhat, clear goggles shielding her amber eyes,
she welded Pressed Steel's boxcars outside Pittsburgh

        like women in Toledo hauling Jeep parts to Ford lines,
        like those assembling fuselages on bombers in Long Beach
        or for Boeing's Flying Fortresses in Seattle,
        like women filing bullets for the Army
        or building ships at California's Richmond docks,
        like those feeding blast furnaces in steel mills,
        sparks flying at the giant cauldrons of molten steel.

        Liberty Girls—the women on railroads, in shipyards,
        as pipe fitters and riggers, bus drivers and mechanics,
        like those shooting riveting guns or ferrying planes,
        ratcheting with wrenches or lighting torches,
        arms linked across America with the plains women,
        with the farm women, the desert and mountain women,
        with the city women, even with Marilyn Monroe
        who, as Norma Jean, attached propellers to planes.

My mother never jumped drunken in her clothes
into a fountain like F. Scott Fitzgerald's new women,
but she did drop, donning her mail-order rayon sheath,
from a rowboat into the lake, belting out the high notes
of "Indian Love Call" at a USO picnic. She learned
to love the night shift as a blackout air warden
and became the woman whom I would later blast
for not pulling free from my father's fierce grip.

I have become the woman who no longer wonders
how I dared knuckle into my own fist, raise it high
for rights in rallies and marches for reason and right
because I had a mother who dared give up a job
as a nursemaid for the rail yard and factory,
relinquish the girdle to the rubber drive, who never
threw off the helmet for the apron, and went on
living as if she could do anything—making a fist.

Maria Mazziotti Gillan

AT THE FACTORY WHERE MY MOTHER WORKED

Once when I was seventeen, I visited the factory
where my mother worked. It was on the second floor
up a flight of narrow, rickety stairs, and when I opened
the door, the noise of sewing machines slapped my face.
I searched for my mother in the close-packed row
of women bent over their sewing. The floor manager
picked up one of the pieces my mother had finished,
screamed, "You call this sewing?" and threw the coat
on the floor. The tables were lit by bare light bulbs,
dangling down on cords. I had never seen the place
where my mother worked. She thought we should be
protected from all that was ugly and mean
in the grown-up world. "Children should be children,"
she'd say. "They'll learn trouble soon enough.
We don't need to tell them about it." She did not answer
the floor walker. Instead she bent her head over her sewing,
but not before I saw the shame in her face.

Grace Bauer

MODERN CLOTHING

Bent over Singers like saints
before altars, half the women
I knew sat, row after row, stitching
the pockets, inseams, cuffs and flies
of men's dress trousers and boy's
sports slacks. For forty hours a week
at *Modern Clothing* they labored themselves
into eyestrain and bad backs.
Now and then one of them—
rushed into carelessness—would sew
through her own skin, the relentless machine
piercing three or four times
before her foot winced off the pedal
and the needle, stippled red, came to rest
against her finger bone, drab threads
imbedded in her flesh like a crude tattoo.

Piece Work, they called it. And for years
I saw my future there, hunched like my grandmother,
who worked waistbands and hauled home
bags of scraps she stacked
in closets and corners. Having forgotten
what she was saving for, she continued,
for decades, to save, until the room
we were forced to share left little room
for us, and I developed a need
for space, the urge to discard.

I despised every square inch of cloth
she found a use for: the mismatched
slip-covers and pillow cases, doll clothes
of severe navy serge, the piecemeal wardrobe

she persisted in wearing despite
drawers full of better dresses
she was saving *for good*—an occasion
I realized early on would never be
good enough for her to squander
on something store-bought, not made by her hands.
She died with her hoard still piling up—
a stash of stuff we deemed useless,
carted off to Goodwill, where today I am
searching for a bargain, hoping to find
something *vintage* perhaps, a garment
that has survived long enough to come back
into fashion, a remnant from a stranger's life
I can salvage and put to good use.

Jacqueline Osherow

AMATA

an excerpt from "Above the Casa del Popolo above Firenze"

In Amata's tiny kitchen the television
Blares its badly dubbed Brazilian soap opera
From its perch on the front-load washing machine
Beside a hectic sink of soaking pots.
He's supposed to be a doctor, but he sneaks around
With the sex-starved mistress of a Mafioso.
Is that intelligent? Would you call that intelligent?
And doesn't even guess the twins are his . . .

Mostly deaf, she has to concentrate to hear
And leaves the local women's chosen fabric
Largely untouched as she pays attention.
During the commercials, she chalks in patterns,
Nonchalantly cuts and starts to baste. Her worktable
(So hastily cleared from this evening's meal
That the bread, two napkins and a spoon remain)
Covers all the floor-space in the kitchen
And presses her chair against a windowsill
Piled with whatever fruit's in season—

Not the window with the sweep of trinket Florence
(That's in an unused, unheated room,
And opened just to see who's at the door,
The Palazzo Vecchio and Duomo elaborate
Trimmings on a faint, misshapen pincushion
Crammed with campaniles' tiny needles)
But the one with the view of distant mountains.
The forests above Vallombrosa? I was never clear.

She'll look like a ball children play with on the beach
With all this red and purple on her giant ass
Is her knowing verdict at the next commercial;
She explains that the future wearer of this dress
Is looking, at age forty, for a husband
Neither divorced, nor widowed, nor older than she.
I tell her she'd better look in the cemetery;
That's the only place she's going to find him.

Maybe where you come from, a man like that
Would marry a woman his own age, but not here.
Then she points to a roll of bluish velvet
And says it's for a friend who has affairs;
The friend claims it's less work than getting married:
"Sex, sure, sex. In bed, anything he wants,
But let that bitch his mother iron his underpants . . ."

Takako Arai

WHEN THE MOON RISES

It is the night shift in an abandoned spinning factory
There is only a single light bulb here
The spools of thread turn by themselves
Click go the bobbins
Changed by the machines
It has already been a decade
Since this place shut down
But when the moon rises, it begins to work
Its strange automation
They say soon after the war
A factory worker's hair got tangled
In the machines, killing her
There are things that float here
But this is not the work of ghosts
No
In the factory
There are peculiar habits
That is what I mean
Peculiar habits remain here
An old lady who spun thread
For forty-four years here
Still licks her index finger and twists
Even on her deathbed
She cannot escape that gesture
That must be true in the netherworld too
Since threads are so infinitely thin
The gestures sink into the bodies
Of those who manipulate the machines
They possess them
Look
How the raw silk thread
Is pulled smoothly

From the factory woman's fingers
Then dances endlessly
The factory is that way too
The axle of the spinning wheel
Remembers
The molecules of steel
Hang their heads in the
Direction in which they spin
Then get caught up
Clanging emptily
When the moonlight pours in
It is not just the tide that is full

Emptily
    Emptily
The spinning wheels spin
The threads swim
Through the abandoned factory

Translated from the Japanese by Jeffrey Angles.

Daisy Fried

LITTLE GIRLS WEAVING

*On the road from the Turkish town of Selçuk to the archaeological site of Ephesus
there is a factory where tourists can buy rugs and watch them being made.*

There are little girls weaving when you walk out in the morning,
and little girls weaving when you walk back at night. In weaving,
the hands, which have a thousand angles—bird, mallet, poultice, purse,
signal, letter, clay wad, smoke—are merely pushed by the arms;
the arms are hung upon the back. Sense of balance is required.
       Little girls have that.

In the museum, Cybele stands up with her trophy testicles.
Priapus stands up with his giant cock's burden of fruit. I
believe in this world of heroes. Little girls weaving don't stand up.
Little girls weaving make no sound. You've got to imagine
the gathering sighing sounds. *Ehrr, huhh, ussh.* Small sounds,
kept inside the shell of the skin, inside little girl lungs. Pushed by the arms,
arms hung on the back. Sense of balance is required. Little girls have that.

Luisa A. Igloria

TEN THOUSAND VILLAGES

Five dry gourds to make a musical rattle like water
cascading over stones. Purses made from wealth
discarded by llamas stepping through trails
lined with prickly vines. Soap from the *neem* tree,
fragrance from slippery skins of overripe mangos
stirred in metal vats. Women set them to heat on fires
crackling to life outside a circle of huts. The rainbow
folds of a *serape* next to last season's newspapers,
each page torn and coiled and dipped in glue to make
a set of placemats. My children wander through aisles
almost narrow as jungle paths, patting *papier-mâché*
elephants pedicured with paisley, nativity scenes small
miracles of cornhusk and dimpled grain. All this
jeweled wealth *(oh pretty!)* made from strings and red clay,
from castoff skins, from the blue-green bottoms of cola
bottles, broken into necklaces of raw silver.
Purchase a basket and clothe a child.
A teakwood cabinet with no nails might feed
a mountain community for a month. *How wonderful,*
exclaims a customer, admiring a *salwar kameez*
dyed the colors of the lipstick tree. Part of her forty
dollars will travel across the world and take up the hands
of weaver girls so patiently knotting threads as though
they awaited bridegrooms, tell them their industry has not
been in vain. Fingering transparent domes of food
covers embroidered with colored straw, I remember the year
my whole elementary school raked vegetable plots
behind the convent—Afternoons, in place of PE
or home economics, we turned the soil with makeshift trowels,
scattered seeds and squealed at the slime of earthworms.
For trellises, we drove overlapping stakes into the ground.
For watering cans, we took empty cans of soup

or fruit cocktail and punched holes along the bottom.
When the school year ended, we cheered as pale blue
sweet pea flowers emerged, and the firm jade ovals of tomatoes;
but never paused to wonder who picked them in the summertime,
who boiled pots of conserve or decorated bowls of salad—
all the red we had grown with our hands.

Rosebud Ben-Oni

AT TEN I HELD THE LOOK OF LOCUST

At ten, I held the look of a locust and mothers of tarp and tin
    held closer their unborn in the streets of childpits.

At ten, the Americans came and built a factory for the women
    to work with solvents and a playground for their children.

In August I'd roost on the sheetmetal roof as a bad omen:
    that lazy locust should be devastating fields.

But nothing ever grew in the *colonia.* My devastation, unsimple:
    A pain to say when not plural, shameful place among pests.

I held the look of a locust, black-sunken eyes and long, thin limbs
    so mothers of melting plastic and plywood

scrambled for sawdust from the mouths of razor-wild men.
    Bloody nails wrote the mornings after in pencil lead.

I was unborn again, with look of locust, leather rebellious,
    spinning backwards, in constant omission,
        undid in twitching.

Twenty years later the factory is condemned, but the playground
    Stands with a sign in English: *WARNING:*
        Toxic waste, no playing.

Twenty years later my molted locust skins mark where we've been.
    They are paper-thin but untorn.
        I look through the fine webbing

at yellow vapor of the never born,
    swinging windless,
        all limb.

Melissa Kwasny

INDUSTRY

I worked in a plastics factory when I was nineteen. We manufactured five-gallon jugs that industrial size cooking oil comes in. I was not proud of my work. No one was. We weren't proud of the paycheck either: two dollars and fifty cents an hour. It was assembly line work. We stood for two hours in one spot, ripping forms from the plastic background they were cast from, slicing the faulty ones with utility knives and sending them back into the forge, burning our fingers. The air was blurry with white plastic particles, like the plankton and plankton-like plastic that clouds the waters of the oceans now.

We waited for our two fifteen minute breaks and our lunch (a sandwich and a cigarette). No windows anywhere. American Plastics, it was called. American Plastics, American Rubber, American Home Foods. National Rubber. All those factories closed down now. Shame of plastic and the married salesmen. Burnt smell of it, perfume spread on toast. Men passing out in the foundry. Women with curlers, at work on the assembly line. No one suggested masks or ear plugs. What the American workplace did to everyone in the 1960s. Good place to get a job, better than fawning, for a girl, better than secretarying.

Shame at not understanding until later. In balloons: what the sea says. What the landfill says. Shame at our bigness, ugliness, now age. Shame at our shameless grab for attention. That we must stand taller. That we can forget names. That we are increasingly left to our own devices. Over-rounding the corners, over-praised. Where is the life within this one once we've erased it? When we think of ourselves in the future tense, already gone? God-particles, thus. Almost eternal.

Elaine Terranova

IN THE BINDERY

The shift begins. Metal clanks
against metal. It's the sound
of a thousand Houdinis shackling
themselves. Over this, the women
go on talking. They understand
each well enough.
"I fell down the stairs. I had
to have it fixed." The other
can't help wondering if her husband
broke her nose. If she had
the operation for her looks.
She's a student. This is
real life to her, this summer job,
while Lena's here for good.
All night the two step out
in small, one-sided pirouettes.
They lift the paper onto
its cradle on the belt, where it
will be trimmed and stapled
farther on. At each step
something is added or taken away.
The steel hands meet unhurriedly,
over and over, at right angles.
The women count on this and on
the short dead points that come
in anyone's life. "Chicken,"
Lena calls. "Don't work
so hard. They don't give medals
here." It's true her muscles ache.
This is the first time they've
been put to any use. She feels
the sweat that stands out

on her forehead like a seal.
Lena is staring straight ahead,
gray eyes like two clear lights.
These were machines, you never
tempted them. Where they held
and supported, they could crush.
The metal rings with force and clarity.
Sometimes it seems to have
a change of heart but then goes on.

Karen J. Weyant

BEAUTY TIPS FROM THE GIRLS ON 3ᴿᴰ SHIFT

Brillo pads get rid of most of the dirt on your hands.
And Lever soap. Forget Ivory or Olay. Hand cream
covers the smell of hot dust, of metal. Try Country Apple
or Passionate Peach. Some girls like the smell of lavender.

Wear red polish. Color hides dark stains and dirt,
especially grime that gets pushed back where hard nail
meets soft skin, that place a metal file can't find.

Wear light foundation. Water-based. It keeps your pores
free from dirt. But don't bother with loose powder.
The dust in the air will take care of the shine.

Forget eyeliner. It will stain the shadows beneath your eyes.
Forget mascara. It will run. Even the waterproof kind.
And don't wear lipstick. Ever. Chapstick will do.

Vaseline is even better. But Cover Girl, Revlon, even Almay
sucks all moisture from your lips, making your smile,
like the rest of you, crack.

Lytton Bell

ANOTHER DAY AT THE DILDO FACTORY

Twenty immigrants in
twenty hairnets
are painting veins on
twenty prosthetic penises

The penises had ceased to seem shocking
to them after just one eight-hour shift,
even to the Catholics,
and they disregard them, gossiping
and chatting amongst themselves
same as if it were only
the paper factory or the ideology factory instead

The penises, molded in a malleable rubber
sway a little
when you touch them
as if to ask:

What are you doing to me?
Where are you sending me?
What will I be doing one week from today?
What is my purpose in this world?
Is there a God?

Finally, one worker says
to one of the penises
Don't ask me, I just work here; I'm only
making minimum wage

Arlitia Jones

SHIT JOB

The machine sucks
and blows in and out
like a yes-man courting money
and all day you catch
what falls out the other end—
meat Cryovac-ed in shiny plastic
pouches you separate out and stack
on racks—the bright red roasts
and beef steaks, the chops and chops,
the chops, the chops. All day.
This. And the warning sign:
AMPUTATION DANGER!
above the hydraulic knife
that slices the film. You read it
a thousand times every day,
each time your hand knocks
against the plastic guard
protecting it. Read again
and make of it what you can:
GREAT DAMNATION!
DANG! A PERMUTATION
TAMPON AND GUITAR or
PURE MAN ATTAIN GOD and even
NO DAMN PIG TREAT!
Otherwise you'd go nuts
and, god forbid, tell the boss
to fuck himself when
the sarcastic sonofabitch sidles up
real friendly like one of the boys
when you enter the dark of the freezer.
He catches the smirk on your face,
MUTANT DOG!

AMPUTATE GONAD!
GO EAT AN ARMPIT!
Anything to keep from hearing
when he leans into your ear
to remind you: *I'd get
a monkey to do your job,
if I could just keep it
from shittin' on the floor.*

Eugenia Toledo

STORIES OF WOMEN

From the margin / from the window ledge
like an ashen butterfly / I went by your side of the street

Sitting in the doorway of your house
you are sniffing the air like an ancient cat

Roaming the streets / ringing the bell
of the place where you work

I saw you at the far end of a garden
scrubbing clothes by hand in a washtub

Begging between cars
dodging those inevitable swells

Your son in your arms
magnifying your low degree

I saw you navigating the night
sparks rising from the spurs of your high heels

Protesting with voices and banners
brandishing your demands and your eyes in the strike

I saw you buying used clothing
as if it were hard candy in your mouth

I knew you were a worker on the 12-hour shift
in the chill of the fish processing and the packing plant

I know that they found you dead
worth less than a sparrow

And I know you have lost your smile
while you make all the necessary preparations

for life and death
Sailing this river full of silt

wounded on every side
seeking a port of fireflies

Barbara LaMorticella

TOYBOX

1.

Big loopy letters dotted with hearts.
Such childish, feminine handwriting
and such heavy consequences . . .

The insurance examiner's signature.

2.

The client sewed 5000 gunnysacks a day
for a whole year, and now can't
use her hands. But we deny her claim.

A single mother with three children
in an unheated trailer in the winter—
Why should the company pay for her operation?

We know that she carried water and firewood.
By the time she started at the factory,
she was already a cracked plate.

3.

The examiner goes home at night
and relaxes with movies. She likes the ones where
ordinary-looking people are really secret aliens,

And the one where, inside the darkness of
toyboxes, pretty dolls turn to cannibals,
begin gnashing their tiny teeth.

Judith Roche

SERIOUS CHILDHOOD

My first memories are of walking a picket line.
Somewhere I sit on the steps of a downtown building.
I am very small.
We are singing *Solidarity Forever*. My mother
keeps me away from angels and Madonna pictures
and fears the nun's fervor in my eyes.
She is not Catholic.
Her high dare was to cross a picket line,
drop, secretly
a stink bomb, perfect and round,
crushing in its paper bag.
The department store crowd
scattered and screamed
and she loved her *braveness*.
I still loved angels but thought
she was one.
She talked about freedom and dignity:
I saw a solitary riverside
where I turned myself into a mermaid.
My mother sang, "Just like a tree a-standing by the water,
we shall not be moved."
We were serious in those days.
She took me to see the Diego Rivera mural at the art museum,
car factory workers full of sweat and muscle strain.
She said rich people didn't believe
working people worked that hard.
I looked at the angel pictures.
We both meant it.

Susana H. Case

BROADS

If we could just get rid of these broads, we'd have it made.

—*Arizona Department of Public Safety officer, 1983*

Four hundred troopers,
seven units of the National Guard—no one
thought the strike would last years.

The first of July, the 5 a.m. shift and soon
desert summer will again scorch into bones.
Broads outside the house
block traffic, are tear-gassed.
When paychecks vanish, the pickup truck,

the striped couch—broads always
show up to picket,
past the heaped sand blockade discarded at the gate,
wild-eyed broads, scar-faced broads,
fat broads, skinny broads,
a mile-long line of broads,
male scabs pulling down twill slacks to show
broads what they lack.

Their pit work, broads
using a jackhammer, cleaning out the stack,
broads in the arsenic holes,
skin turning green where the paper coverall rips.
They can do heavy lifting too.

Broads outside the house—without male
permission!—As if

they were hookers, *without morals,*
without muscle,

as if each were nobody.

In 1983, Arizona was the site of a copper mine strike in which the management of Phelps Dodge Corporation decided to try to break the union, which had a number of women members who took part in the worker resistance. The strike lasted nearly three years, and Phelps Dodge succeeded in decertifying the union, a significant defeat for the American labor movement. Soon after the union was broken, copper prices soared, as did Phelps Dodge's profits.

Dorianne Laux

WHAT I WOULDN'T DO

The only job I didn't like, quit
after the first shift, was selling
subscriptions to *TV Guide* over the phone.
Before that it was fast food, all
the onion rings I could eat, handing
sacks of deep fried burritos through
the sliding window, the hungry hands
grabbing back. And at the Laundromat,
plucking bright coins from a palm
or pressing them into one, kids
screaming from the bathroom and twenty
dryers on high. Cleaning houses was fine,
polishing the knick-knacks of the rich.
I liked holding the hand-blown glass bell
from Czechoslovakia up to the light,
the jeweled clapper swinging lazily
from side to side, its foreign,
A-minor ping. I drifted, an itinerant,
from job to job, the sanatorium
where I pureed peas and carrots
and stringy beets, scooped them,
like pudding, onto flesh-colored
plastic plates, or the gas station
where I dipped the ten-foot measuring stick
into the hole in the blacktop, pulled it up hand
over hand into the twilight, dripping
its liquid gold, pink-tinged.
I liked the donut shop best, 3 AM,
alone in the kitchen, surrounded
by sugar and squat mounds of dough,
the flashing neon sign strung from wire
behind the window, gilding my white uniform

yellow, then blue, then drop-dead red.
It wasn't that I hated calling them, hour
after hour, stuck in a booth with a list
of strangers' names, dialing their numbers
with the eraser end of a pencil and them
saying hello. It was that moment
of expectation, before I answered back,
the sound of their held breath,
their disappointment when they realized
I wasn't who they thought I was,
the familiar voice, or the voice they loved
and had been waiting all day to hear.

Elaine Sexton

CLASS

I lasted three days minding a child
at the beach club on a thin strand
of sand, where my family lived
but did not belong. I took over the job

my sisters had before me,
my sisters, who sat every summer,
gladly, reading books, getting tans,
earning money for college.

On the second day I knelt by the pool,
the north Atlantic in sight,
the Isles of Shoals raised clearly
in the distance. I watched a girl

not much younger than I swimming
laps. The sun bleached the water
in the pool, licking its sides
the way my soft drink

licked my glass. Idle, like the idle rich
parents at the bar, I watched this girl
as if reading would be stealing
the attention they paid for. This was

my lesson. Back and forth she swam,
back and forth I weighed belonging
& not belonging, the salt water,
always free, the steps to it, already mine.

Lucia Perillo

FIRST JOB/SEVENTEEN

Gambelli's waitresses sometimes got down on their knees,
searching for coins dropped into the carpet—
hair coiled stiff, lips coated in that hennaed shade of red,
the banner-color for lives spent in the wake of husbands
dying without pensions, their bodies used in ceaseless
marching toward the kitchen's dim mouth, firm legs
migrating slowly ankleward. From that kitchen doorway,
Frankie Gambelli would sic a booze-eye on them,
his arms flapping in an earthbound pantomime of that
other Frank: The Swooned-Over. "You old cunts,"
he'd mutter. "Why do I put up with you old cunts?"—
never managing to purge his voice's tenor note
of longing. At me—the summer girl—he'd only stare
from between his collapsing red lids, eyes that were empty.

Once I got stiffed on a check when a man jerked crazy-faced
out of his seat, craned around, then bolted
from those subterranean women, sweaty and crippled
in the knees. Though I chased him up the stairs to the street,
the light outside was blinding and I lost the bastard
to that whiteness, and I betrayed myself with tears.
But coming back downstairs my eyes dried on another vision:
I saw that the dusk trapped by the restaurant's plastic greenery
was really some residual light of that brilliance happening
above us on the street. Then for a moment the waitresses
hung frozen in midstride—cork trays outstretched—
like wide-armed, reeling dancers, the whole
some humming and benevolent machine that knew no past, no future—
only balanced glasses, and the good coin in the pocket.
Sinatra was singing "Jealous Lover." All of us were young.

Madeline DeFrees

ON MY SIXTIETH BIRTHDAY,
I WORK AT THE YELLOW SUN

Sunday. I am mopping up spills in the oils with the young.
On time as I begin my next iambic decade
making poems in the cooler of the universal co-op. Never won
an NEA, a Guggenheim, a handout from the American
Council of Learned Societies, the NEH, or the Rockefeller
fellers.

   In spite of villanelles beside the shallow bird
feeder, I consider the anapests, how they grow
among the ruminant Final Readers. Happy out of habit,
cutting the big cheeses, I ask myself how they
age so rich in rhyme, too highly seasoned for my taste,
when I must step carefully past the elbow
macaroni and real bristle brushes
merely to get by.

     We are all workers here. We do not
qualify for easy money, fenugreek and choriamb, cheap yogurt,
the perennial sestina. I weave through dead legumes: split
pea and lentil, the beans—soy, kidney, lima. Steep
yogi tea in my head amid the crush of tarragon and cloves,
coriander, cardamom, lemon verbena. My jeans
flourish among the sprouts and peanuts, the whole
grains and dried fruits, the pure clover
honey of the Yellow Sun.

      Still it would be nice to win
a free ride on the mood elevator with the Yale
lock. To step inside the Critics Circle, charmed by
a second's look, board a surface train for Coquilles
St. Jacques and the Pulitzer, break the downhill

cycle of trochees and dactyls. ("Never make it big by
pedaling.") Next stop, the Nobel. Forget
the Lamont people. A Calimyrna fig to the fickle
trustees of inflated dollars for the PSA
in any form or freedom.

                    In my sixtieth November, let me
stay, not straining gnats beside the shrill
menstrual sponges, the colanders and paring knives,
regalia of the Bard-behind-the-Grille. Try
Khadrawi dates on a Little Magazine rather than
blush unseen. Milk the unpasteurized
editor for all he can give, haywagon pried from the stars.
Better late (and less) than inorganic

                          sour grapes. Let me
sprint to a lyrical finish out-of-print, a modest
royalty. Not given a riotous living, I'll take
twenty years more behind bars—sunlight and music—roses
and muses, prisoner of the Yellow Sun.

Kate Lebo

LEMON MERINGUE

Legend has it lemon meringue pie was invented by the Sisters of the Holy Names the day after their first night in Portland, Oregon. On the day of the invention of lemon meringue pie, clouds gathered overhead, all threat and no spit, just a cluster of gray over sun. Back east, the sisters had heard tales of Exodus-style rains, flooding until the future courthouse and city hall were specks of marble flotsam only God could pinch from the froth. Sister Maria in her tent, contemplating a month of daylight darkness ahead, remembered the seven lemons in her trunk. She squeezed them into yolks and sugar, then poured the filling into an improvised crust of crackers. Taking inspiration from her new home's dour weather, she beat sweetened egg whites until they puffed like clouds and gently piled them over the bright yellow filling, obscuring it from view.

The sisters loved her creation and fought for the biggest pieces. Sister Maria disliked the sound of raised voices, so she walked into the woods to leave the din behind. As she peered through dripping firs for a glimpse of construction further upriver, she thought about God and said, "You don't want pie in the sky when you die. You want something here on the ground while you're still around."

Years later, unbeknownst to them both, Muhammad Ali would say the exact same thing after winning a fight in Miami. The sisters campaigned to make this aphorism the motto of the school for girls they planned to construct, and though Home Economics is considered unfeminist and unfashionable these days, some still think that St. Mary's Academy for Girls should complement their rigorous math and science courses with a lesson on how to whip the perfect whites.

Shannon Camlin Ward

LEARNING TO WAIT

To balance plates between the elbow and the wrist, stack with your dominant hand. Make sure the palm of the other is upturned, and stretch the arm to a flat line. No, not with oatmeal the first time. Here are some fries. They're cheap. Use those. They won't make such a mess when you drop them. Now take a step, slow. Oops, there they go! Did I mention it's a dollar per broken plate? When you write the tickets, abbreviate if you want to keep up. No, HB is hamburger, not hash browns. Did I mention you'll have to pay for that? When the orders take too long, don't apologize. It makes 'em more apt to think it ought to be free. Use Soft Scrub to bleach the rings of iced tea from the tables, and clean the coffee pots with salt and ice. Double knot your apron strings so perverts can't untie them. Look, you can spend all day sulking or suck it up. This place is a goldmine if you can hack it.

Sarah Freligh

WAITRESS

after Dorianne Laux

Wednesdays I waited on women golfers, endless
four tops just in from playing
a hot eighteen. They drank gallons
of unsweetened iced tea, demanded refills

for free and complained when the brew
wasn't cold or strong enough.
I ran on cans of Tab,
kept a lit Newport perched in the crotch

of a black ashtray, lucky to get
three deep drags between cocktails
and order ups. The grill cook pointed
a knife at me, threatened to cut off

my tits if I didn't speak up. The bartender
screamed at me for garnishing
a dry Manhattan with a maraschino cherry.
I leaned on the roll warmer and cried.

No one paid attention. Every week, at least,
someone untied her black apron and said
Fuck it, walked out in the middle of a shift
never to be seen again. I dried my eyes.

In the nineteenth hole men slipped bills
in my pocket, eyed the V-neck
of my uniform whenever I set down
another round. An hour after my shift,

I was shit-faced in a bar that didn't card me,
paying for cold Molsons with quarters left
by the lady golfers. I don't remember
walking home on those nights, only

the mornings when I woke to a wink
of coins on the bureau, hours before
I had to punch a clock again.

Thylias Moss

ONE-LEGGED COOK

A high school cafeteria
is where I work. "Hop to it, Velma,"
kids say when the line moves slow.
My son eats outdoors from a bag,
collar turned up, napkin
covering his knees.
That's what I live with.
Never occurred to me
I was missing out on something.
Though seldom seen in Culvert Hall
I know to sit still
when the conductor taps his stick;
my mother waved a strap.
Besides, it doesn't take that much,
the burdock by the courthouse
grew an eighth of an inch
since yesterday.
A lot of folks didn't notice.

Patti Sullivan

DOG EAT DOG

1970

My bullet-proof nylon uniform
was usually covered with a splatter of chili
polish sausage grease and milkshake mix

I foolishly kept the stainless steel bun steamers
clean and shining like mirrors
while the two high school boys working there
spent their shift throwing a football around in the parking lot

Our manager spent most of her time
driving from franchise to franchise
leaving her mangy collie tied up in the store room all day
I took pity on the poor thing and once in a while
brought him fake strawberry milkshakes

My fast food-career lasted almost a year
ending on a dramatic note
I was the victim of one of the oldest tricks in the book

So the customer gives me a twenty-dollar bill
apologizes for having nothing smaller
for his seventy-five-cent coffee
I gave him nineteen dollars and twenty-five cents change

He takes the coffee, his change and starts to leave
turns back to me and says, "Oh, I had a dollar after all
so here you go—just give me back my twenty"

So I do and he leaves with his twenty
my nineteen dollars and twenty-five cents
and the coffee

The manager almost had me talked into paying her back for the loss

I quit instead—she'd have to get somebody else
maybe one of those high school boys
to keep her drive-thru window spotless

It wouldn't be me.

Nikky Finney

LABOR STRIKE

Black girl
bobbin' on the Wednesday street,
McDonald's pencil
layin' back
'cross her ear,
like she ain't at work
and heretofore
from now on
for evermore
is refusin' to take
your orders.

Sandra Beasley

VOCATION

For six months I dealt Baccarat in a casino.
For six months I played Brahms in a mall.
For six months I arranged museum dioramas;
my hands were too small for the Paleolithic
and when they reassigned me to lichens, I quit.
I type ninety-one words per minute, all of them
Help. Yes, I speak Dewey Decimal.
I speak Russian, Latin, a smattering of Tlingit.
I can balance seven dinner plates on my arm.
All I want to do is sit on a veranda while
a hard rain falls around me. I'll file your 1099s.
I'll make love to strangers of your choice.
I'll do whatever you want, as long as I can do it
on that veranda. If it calls you, it's your calling,
right? Once I asked a broker what he loved
about his job, and he said *Making a killing.*
Once I asked a serial killer what made him
get up in the morning, and he said *The people.*

Denise Duhamel

UNEMPLOYMENT

from *Recession Commandments*

for six days thou shalt labor and do all thy work
for six days thou shalt post thy resume, hand deliver thy resume,
     rewrite thy resume to best suit labor sought, mail thy resume
     overnight or priority, fudge thy resume
for six days thou shalt kept track of all thy efforts to qualify for an extension
     of unemployment benefits
for six days thou shalt feel guilty, cry, wring thy hands, redo thy checkbook,
     pawn thy TV and thy jewelry
for six days thou shalt fill out applications at chain restaurants, hospitals,
     retail stores, schools, offices of all types (including temp offices),
     banks, nail salons, hair salons, supermarkets, nursing homes,
     construction sites, topless bars, hotdog stands
for six days thou shalt set up an e-bay account to sell thy dishes,
     and thou shalt bring thy best clothes to a consignment shop
for six days thou shalt call up favors and let go of thy pride
for six days thou shalt apply for no-interest credit cards
for six days thou shalt fill out applications to become a telemarketer,
     a customer service employee, a tutor, a nanny, a janitor, a maid,
     a dog-walker, a dogcatcher, a cashier, a mail order bride
for six days thou shalt write letters to government officials when unemployment
     extension benefits are denied
for six days thou shalt labor and do all the work thou can find

Sharon Hashimoto

FOUR WEEKS UNEMPLOYED:
I FAIL THE WATER DEPARTMENT'S
LIFT AND CARRY EXAM

My cheek feels the rough touch—
burlap hugged close in my arms.
A man repeats the warning:
Lift with your legs, not your back.

Burlap hugged close in my arms,
I raise 30 pounds of soil to the table,
lifting with my legs, not my back.
The shifting sack has no bottom.

How to raise 40 pounds of soil to a table?
I balance the weight on my hip.
The shifting sack shapes a bottom
on the ledge of bone. I stumble—

unbalanced. The weight on my hip
wants to return to the earth, spill
over the ledge of bone. Stumbling,
my breath collapses like skins of small balloons

wanting to return to the earth, spilled
of their air. At 50 pounds, my body knows its limits.
My breath collapses like skins of small balloons
holding everything together. But I can't escape

beyond a body's limits.
I want a job, a secure position
to hold everything together. I can't escape
the words of my mother and father:

You need a job, they say, a secure position.
Late nights, I fell asleep listening
to the words of my mother and father.
When did they let go of their dreams?

Late nights, did they fall asleep listening
to each drop of rain breaking against the roof,
remember how the sky let go of its dreams?
I pulled the illusion of warmth close to my body,

folded myself into rain breaking against the roof.
My cheek feels the rough touch
of burlap. Two minutes to finish,
a man repeats the warning.

Natasha Trethewey

LETTER HOME

New Orleans, November 1910

Four weeks have passed since I left, and still
I must write to you of no work. I've worn down
the soles and walked through the tightness
of my new shoes calling upon the merchants,
their offices bustling. All the while I kept thinking
my plain English and good writing would secure
for me some modest position. Though I dress each day
in my best, hands covered with the lace gloves
you crocheted—no one needs a *girl*. How flat
the word sounds, and heavy. My purse thins.
I spend foolishly to make an appearance of quiet
industry, to mask the desperation that tightens
my throat. I sit watching—

though I pretend not to notice—the dark maids
ambling by with their white charges. Do I deceive
anyone? Were they to see my hands, brown
as your dear face, they'd know I'm not quite
what I pretend to be. I walk these streets
a white woman, or so I think, until I catch the eyes
of some stranger upon me, and I must lower mine,
a *negress* again. There are enough things here
to remind me who I am. Mules lumbering through
the crowded streets send me into reverie, their footfall
the sound of a pointer and chalk hitting the blackboard
at school, only louder. Then there are women, clicking
their tongues in conversation, carrying their loads
on their heads. Their husky voices, the wash pots
and irons of the laundresses call to me.

I thought not to do the work I once did, back bending
and domestic; my schooling a gift—even those half days
at picking time, listening to Miss J—. How
I'd come to know words, the recitations I practiced
to sound like her, lilting, my sentences curling up
or trailing off at the ends. I read my books until
I nearly broke their spines, and in the cotton field,
I repeated whole sections I'd learned by heart,
spelling each word in my head to make a picture
I could see, as well as a weight I could feel
in my mouth. So now, even as I write this
and think of you at home, *Goodbye*

is the waving map of your palm, is
a stone on my tongue.

II

THE DUST OF EVERYDAY LIFE

Jana Harris

from THE DUST OF EVERYDAY LIFE

from BOOK FOUR: INK

THOMAS & HELEN HODGSON,
OLYMPIA, WASHINGTON STATE CAPITAL
SWANTOWN LANE, 1890-91

X. (HELEN)

A new house meant I must
take in piece work from
our temperance newsletter
The Echo and, because
I'm one of the few
who knows shorthand,
transcribe election speeches
using the juice of Oregon grape
as ink. Tedious work, but
buys the June perfume
of trillium, sweet pansy faces, and
dogtooth violets
on the shade side of our cottage
where my babies
Eli and Sarah
sleep in dry goods
boxes safe from flies.

II. TEMPERANCE HODGSON WICKE
SPOKANE FALLS, WASHINGTON

SPILLAGE

Husband Howard gone all day
to the bank, golfing on weekends.
I used to caddie for father, but wives
aren't allowed. In high school,
I'd wanted to nurse,
but Father feared the naked
bodies of men would spoil me
for marriage. At the university,
I took a normal degree
and taught near a dying
silver mine. Wild cattle ran
out of bunch grass hills through
sea-of-mud streets to the river.
Nighthawk City, not one painted building.
Some scholars came to school hungry
and without lunch pails. One girl
never wore shoes or coat
and coughed so loudly I couldn't
shout over her. Another couldn't
see the slate no matter how
large the chalk letters.
I took my scholars down to the creek
and cooked fudge every day for a week.
Accused of stealing sugar,
I was fired,
sent home to Olympia, where I set
newspaper type. After too many
proof reading errors,
Mother said I was so keen
with numbers I ought to keep books.
Making bank deposits,
I met my husband.

from BOOK SIX: "COME SIT BY MY SIDE IF YOU LOVE ME," 1933

II. HELEN
LA CONNER, WASHINGTON

I often think of mother's wedding:
A Kentucky girl, fifteen,
clearing land, burning willow
swags, working ash into soil, then
mixing seed and sand
before sowing. At harvest,
tobacco leaves large as children
pulled and hung upside down,
dried, cured, stitched into "hands."
Late spring brought late floods, hail
ruined what crop remained.
Fleeing to Ohio, her people
surprised to find land so wide
and empty, without church or store.

Lois Red Elk

THE KNIFE WEARER

This morning we found ourselves skinning a deer,
cutting meat, hanging some to dry and packaging
some for the freezer. It was the dogs late last night

that set off a howling, the unexpected smell of fresh
blood floating down the block, then a familiar car
horn honking in the driveway. My nephew and his

friends were hunting and brought us a deer. Mother
always said, "Cut up the meat right away, don't let
it sit." I look at a front quarter, a hole filled with

coagulated blood. Grandma says not to eat the part
next to the wound, "Cut it out; offer it to the earth for
healing, a sacrifice to remember the hungering spirits."

Auntie says to save the muscle along the back strap,
"It makes good thread." I carefully learned the exact
place to cut the joints so the bones separate easily.

Mother said that is important—"It means you are a
thoughtful person." Auntie is at the door waiting for
a roast. "An elder takes the first piece," she reminded.

Mom tells me to save the hooves for her. She wants
to make a bone game for the new grandchild, wants
him to be patient and skillful. I boil the hoofs with

sage, find the little toe-bones for her. My hands begin
to ache from the work, I soak them in warm water
and start again. I admire the placement of tendons

on the deer shoulders, no joints, just the crisscrossing
of muscle. Grandma says, "That's why your dad called
them jumpers, they bounce off the strength of their

flexing muscles." Late at night Mom helps me stake
out the hide. My back hurts; my feet feel like I've
been walking on rocks all day. I want to complain,

but Mom catches the look in my eyes. She says to me,
"When you get dressed for the dance this weekend,
you will proudly wear your beautiful beaded dress,

your beaded leggings and moccasins, and last, but not
least, you will put on your beaded belt, and attached
you will wear your sharp knife and quilled knife sheath

because of what you have done this day."

Linda Hogan

WOMAN CHOPPING WOOD

I like the smell of pine
in those rings
of the axe.

Feel the muscles
growing in my arms.

But the fire most always dies out
at three a.m.
cold nights
and I can't hold it
in my arms
alone.

Kathya Alexander

from NAA NAA

She wake up in the blackness. The darkest hour of the day.
Just before the Lord come and roll the nighttime away.
She the color of night. Her skin stretched tight
across her face. And the veins on her hands tell the whole story of her life.

She heish her gown over her head. And she get dressed in the dark.
She run her hand over the few strands of hair she got left.
Then she tie a headwrap around it. And put her straw hat on.
To protect herself from the scorching heat of the sun
that she know is coming. She eat biscuits and molasses for her first meal.
Then she get the beans and cornbread in the tin can that she carry out to the fields
for her lunch. Pretty soon she know the cotton picking truck gone be coming.
She running late this morning. So she know she need to hurry.
It's already after 3 o'clock. She usually ready by now.
She put her hands on her back and she stretch herself out.
She gone be bent over all day long. Her knees is already creaking.
And she thank God that she got knees that still able to bend before him.

She flex her arthritic hands and rub the rheumatiz in her knees.
Then she get her cotton sack from behind the cupboard where she keep it.
Work is her salvation. In Heaven above and down here below.
Work is the only thing that she done ever knowed.
She thank God she can work. For as long as she able.
She go to work when she three to help put food on the table.
That's when she first start chopping cotton. Her mama make her a little hoe.
And she done worked ever since. That was a long time ago.

She pull her stockings on and tie a knot at the knees.
Then she put on her brogans, run over at the heels.
She go sit out on the porch and wait for the cotton truck to come.
In the sky, she look for the first tinge of the sun.
But the sun is still sleeping. Ain't got no need to come up yet.

Ain't nothing out this early but colored folks and the white
folks who carry them to work. The sun come up when it please.
She ain't never in her life done woke up with such ease
as the sun rise in the morning. She think about that song that say,
that lucky old sun that ain't got nothing to do 'cept roam around heaven all day.

Going in and out the rows, that song seem to carry
her on thru the day. Even when her back is breaking.
When the strap digging, and the cotton sack she hauling is weighing
more than she do. She always pick more than 800 pounds.
She a little bitty woman. No bigger than a 10 year old child.

She fly thru the rows which is longer than a mile.
Her hands flying thru the bolls, sweat falling in her eyes.
She wipe the sweat off her brow with the kerchief round her neck.
She pick her first 100 lbs before the sun even up.
By the time the sun hang straight up in the sky,
she be near 500 lbs and so tired she almost crying.
Some folks try to trick the scales. Put dirt and rocks in they sack.
But she proud that she always do a honest day's work.

Lam Thi My Da

NIGHT HARVEST

White circles of conical hats have come out
Like the quiet skies of our childhood
Like an egret's spreading wings in the night
White circles evoking the open sky

The golds of rice and cluster-bombs blend together
Even delayed-fuse bombs bring no fear
Our spirits have known many years of war
Come, sisters, let us gather the harvest

Each of us wears her own small moon
Glittering on a carpet of gold rice
We are the harvesters of my village
Twelve white hats bright in the long night

We are not frightened by bullets and bombs in the air
Only by dew wetting our lime-scented hair

Translated from the Vietnamese by Martha Collins and Thuy Dinh

Donna J. Gelagotis Lee

THE OLIVE GROVE

painting, Lésvos, Greece

I follow that girl
into the olive grove,
where men force the fruit
out of the limbs with long
hand-carved poles they balance,
like tightrope walkers
edging farther and farther out
on the arms of the trees,
while the women pick up each fleshy
globe from the unyielding ground,
their daughters joining them,
their kerchiefed heads
like the smooth skins
of olives, hands covered
with soil. But *this* girl, it seems,
will walk right through
the grove, freed
by the trees themselves as they stand
persistent, resolute in the years
anchoring them to the soil,
determined to endure,
as if they could raise their arms
and defy the men—to
come, shake these branches,
see what will fall—
and *she* would walk to the other
side of that grove, having never
picked the bitter still-green fruit,
having never knelt beneath the men
to face the hard earth and a web of nets.

Diana García

COTTON ROWS, COTTON BLANKETS

Sprawled on the back of a flatbed truck
we cradled hoes, our minds parceling rows
of cotton to be chopped by noon. Dawn stuck
in the air. Blackbirds rang the willows.

Ahead, a horse trailer stretched across the road.
Braced by youth and lengths of summer breeze
we didn't give a damn. We'd be late, we joked,
stalled by a pregnant mare draped in sheets.

Later, backs to the sun, bandanas tied
to shade our brows, hands laced with tiny cuts;
later, when the labor contractor
worked us through lunch without water; our dried
tongues cursed that mare in cotton blankets
brought to foal in the outlines of summer.

Linda M. Hasselstrom

CLARA: IN THE POST OFFICE

I keep telling you, I'm not a feminist.
I grew up an only child on a ranch,
so I drove tractors, learned to ride.
When the truck wouldn't start, I went to town
for parts. The man behind the counter
told me I couldn't rebuild a carburetor.
I could: every carburetor on the place. That's
necessity, not feminism.
                              I learned to do the books
after my husband left me and the debts
and the children. I shoveled show and pitched hay
when the hired man didn't come to work.
I learned how to pull a calf
when the vet was too busy. As I thought
the cow did most of it herself; they've been
birthing alone for ten thousand years. Does
that make them feminists?
                              It's not
that I don't like men: I love them—when I can.
But I've stopped counting on them
to change my flats or open my doors.
That's not feminism; that's just good sense.

Ana Maria Spagna

THE ONLY GIRL ON THE TRAIL CREW

Pick it up.

Unless you run the saw, you aren't for real. You can dig back bent with a Pulaski through layers of duff. You can chop roots thick as legs. You can pry boulders with a bar or pound them with a sledge, hump half your weight on your back, sleep in the dirt in the rain. As long as the guys run the saw and you swamp for them—that is, you roll the logs they buck off the trail, day after day, and carry their gas and wedges and axe like a caddy—you're not for real.

So pick it up. No one will hand it to you.

Try it at home. Pull the starter, again and again, until your fingers bleed. Pinch the bar and throw the chain. Time the undercut so the once-tree drops clean. Sharpen the teeth, and file the rakers, blow out the filter, adjust the carburetor. Repeat.

Now it's time. Throw the saw on your shoulder on a horse blanket scrap, and hike to the first downed log. Drop your pack, set the choke, pull the cord, dig the dogs in thick bark and sink the bar. The guys will wait to swamp the logs you buck.

This world, these woods are yours.

Ten miles, twenty. Fifteen years, more. You've barber-chaired maples, hung-up cedars, clogged the exhaust, drank yourself sick, swore yourself rank, reheated coffee, shared your gin, shat behind root wads, singed your hair. Earplugs in the washer and cramps in the night and you know it's time, but you can't do it. Without it you weren't real. So what now?

Put it down.

Holly J. Hughes

WORKING ON DECK

Coil the line down *against the sun*
    the old timers said,
clockwise on deck,
    and ten years later
my arms still breaststroke
    the familiar movement
loop upon loop
    rolling the line a quarter turn
against kinks,
    feeling the resistance
give way in my hands,
    stiff fibers yielding:
the line knows how to lay
    if you let it.

Now all the old loops come back
    and my hands swim
down the line by heart
    and the line remembers
all its lives,
    the past firm
in its fibers,
    how they intertwine
coil upon coil
    circling emptiness,
all to make way for the next.

Erin Fristad

ADVICE TO FEMALE DECKHANDS

You will be the cook.
In addition to wheel watches, working
on deck, unloading fish, fueling up,
filling fresh water, mending nets,
grocery shopping whenever you come to town,
you will also prepare three meals a day
and two hearty snacks to go with coffee.
You must keep the kettle on the stove full
and the juice jug and two gallons of milk in the fridge.

You will learn to slice vegetables, prepare a marinade,
cook pasta and fillet a salmon
in twenty minute intervals
while the net is out. You will learn
to ignore the other crew members sitting
at the galley table reading. You must know
how to create a corral in rough weather,
so pots of soup don't end up dripping
down the firewall behind the stove. You will need
bungie cords to keep the cast iron skillet from sliding.
These cords melt if they touch the stovetop.
Keep a squeeze container of Aloe Vera gel
under the galley sink for the burns
on your hands and forearms.

The stove will blow out on windy days
when you're exhausted,
your skin stinging with jellyfish.
The crew will say they're not hungry on these days
but when you slide behind the Cape, it will be flat
calm and all of you will be starving.
Before relighting the stove

determine how much diesel has built up.
If it's more than an inch deep,
turn off the fuel source
by flipping a breaker in the engine room.
You don't have time for ear protection. Get down there
and back before someone hollers for you on deck.
Passing the engine, watch the straps on your raingear,
your ponytail, where you put your hands.

When cooking, remember all odors from the galley
drift directly into the wheelhouse. Fish sauce
smells like dirty tennis shoes. Once she smells this,
your skipper's daughter will refuse to eat anything
she suspects has fish sauce. As a woman and cook
you will be expected to have a special bond
with the skipper's daughter
and you will. Have art supplies in a shoebox in the galley,
a drawing tablet under a cushion, collect starfish,
Decorator crab, and Spiny Lump Suckers in a deck bucket.
Teach her what you know can kill her. When she cries
put your arm around her, kiss her
on the top of the head and let her cry.
Allow her to use your cell phone to call friends
in exchange for making salads, pots of coffee,
washing lunch dishes, carrying groceries to the boat.
Develop sign language for communicating
when she stands in the galley door
peering out at you on deck.

This isn't what I intended.
I set out to give you advice for taking care
of yourself, now it's about taking care of a girl
you're related to by circumstance.
This is exactly what will happen.
You'll notice a hum
more penetrating than the engine.

Susan Eisenberg

PARTNER #3

She smelled dynamite on his shirt;
men on the crew noticed
nothing peculiar.
She moved cautiously, lit
no matches. When she turned him down
for an after-work drink she heard the fuse

ignite. He stopped
calling her by name, just *Waitress!*
and gave his coffee order in strict
detail   Bagel toasted   Not grilled
            Orange juice   With ice
Whenever an elevator door closed leaving them
alone for a caged ride he recounted
hunting stories: deer drenched in blood. Still
like his too-conscious politeness or his
eerily frozen smile these were hardly
sufficient evidence—he a journeyman, she
an apprentice—for complaining out of place.

The afternoon he threatened death
by strangulation
            for the nurse
            and the medical director's wife
reciting their crimes (so like her own) as he
stared into her face, the whole while throwing
retrieving, throwing, retrieving, throwing
an open knifeblade against a wooden ladder,
staring, staring into her face
as he threw the open knife that day

she risked   requesting a transfer.

67

Maria Termini

CHANDELIER

Awkward carrying that fourteen-foot ladder,
excavated out of the junk-filled basement,
I fish it up narrow stairs and around corners,
into the small square space of the hallway,
careful but still the ladder bumps the chandelier.

Today I am repairing water damage.
I climb to a sixteen-foot cathedral ceiling,
on an aluminum ladder that wobbles.
If I had wings, I'd feel so relaxed
but I don't look down and there is work to do.
The chandelier is inches from my nose,
covered with fuzzy dust only I can see.

Meanwhile rusty stains from melting snow
bloom where the ceiling meets the wall,
plaster has cracked and bubbled in spots.
I balance with one hand on the door trim,
the other scraping loose plaster—sanding, patching,
up and down moving the ladder to other spots,
careful but still the ladder bumps the chandelier.

The chandelier is a preposterous affair,
circles of green glass form a wedding cake
that sways like an ominous pendulum—
hanging from one weakening wire,
creaking like the defined ticking of a clock.
It could crash at any moment,
ricochet off the ladder,
slicing my face into noodles,

and it would be my fault.
I would have to pay for it,
and surely it's expensive.

I work through the morning,
respecting the chandelier,
careful but still the ladder bumps the chandelier.

I snake the ladder back into the basement,
replace the pictures on the walls.

As I leave the job, the chandelier messes with me,
I see a trace of its slow mocking dance,
but we have an agreement that when it crashes down,
I won't be around.

Davi Walders

WORKING WONDERS

Oseola McCarty (1908-1999) donated $150,000 in 1995
to establish an endowed scholarship fund for needy students
at the University of Southern Mississippi,
after never earning more than $9,000 a year.

So large, so real, so present,
Oseola McCarty might just speak
from the Annie Leibovitz portrait
in the museum gallery. Sweaters
a-kilter, hair a crown of uncontrolled
silver, she stares into the camera,
lips set, almost smiling. She stands
in Hattiesburg heat, her yard and
wood-frame house a background blur
behind her large eyes and steady gaze.

So many nevers—never finished
Eureka Elementary, never drove,
never traveled, never explored
or earned more than nine thousand
dollars each of the seventy-five
years she took in laundry before
arthritis crippled her. Washing
each dropped-off bundle, ironing,
folding, tying up her small deposits
week after week, year after year.

And then the decision. Summoning up
a vision from her own deprivation. Walking
to the bank, making the withdrawal.
The long, slow bus trip across town.
Waiting. Waiting all afternoon
to startle, to hand over one hundred

fifty thousand dollars to Southern Miss.
Waiting to speak, to give, to educate
others. Waiting with that same look
as she stands in her level yard,
her level eyes daring you to cry.

Vandana Khanna

EARNING AMERICA

I started with minimum wage
in between stacks of government
documents, large prints,

and mysteries. I alphabetized,
straightened spines, stamped backs.
Then came the shoveling—

sun-burnt, smelling sweet
and bitter all at the same time,
digging my way past tiny

apartments in my old
neighborhood, where rows
of men lined the sidewalks

with their shadows. My mother
never worked before America,
planned her days around

cooking classes and shopping
at South Extension for silk saris
and bangles, sharing cold coffee

with her sisters. Here, she spent
nights in the airport cafeteria,
sweeping floors free of napkins,

wrappers, pieces of bread.
She came home at dawn
to roll out dough, boil eggs

in a pot. Oceans away,
her father bided his time:
threw garden parties,

collected newspaper
clippings about America—
his life's work spread out

in the neat columns
of the newspaper,
in the constant attention

to a world he could only
imagine. Never knowing
the day-to-day of cold bus stops

and stubborn typewriters,
of reading want ads. Of working
the Indian out of your voice.

Carolina Hospital

MOURNING DOVES

Each Tuesday, she opens the drapes,
like a tabernacle,
to the trunk of the Sabal Palm,
a criss-cross pattern of spiky leaf bases
splitting the second floor window.

How could she have missed
this hidden nest of twigs and dry grass
as she wiped down the window sill? She asks me.

The doves' soft grays blend with the frond boots.
Anyone could've missed them.

We lean over the granite ledge,
side by side,
gazing at the doves, awed
like toddlers, instead of middle-aged mothers.

It doesn't matter that since she departed
Oaxaca, she has only dusted
strangers' knick-knacks, like mine,
with only a 3rd grade education,
while I inhabit exile
girdled by words. We

wait for the mourning dove nestled above its chick
to move. The tiny beak
peeks from beneath its gray roundness.
The parent shifts to make room
revealing the young speck beneath
its long tapered tail. The mate

lands, opens its mouth wide.
The tiny pigeon, head inside,
feeds from the glandular milk.
Both their necks stir in transfer.

Judith Ayn Bernhard

ADOLFO OR RODOLFO?

"A-dol-fo," he said.
his driver's license
confirmed it

the picture looked
like someone who
might have been
his cousin

"I need a Social
Security Card,"
I said.

he opened his
wallet and took
out a small piece
of paper with nine
digits printed on it

"I need the card,"
I said. "I have to
make a copy."

"Sure," he said.
"Tomorrow."

four days later,
he brought me
an authentic
looking card

even remember
his fake name?

The boss said,
"Where is Rodolfo
working?"

I said, "His name's
Adolfo."

The boss said, "They
call him, Rodolfo."
I said, "His driver's
license says, Adolfo,
he told me, Adolfo."

The boss said, "I
don't want to
hear about it."

I asked Adolfo what
his name is

he seemed to be
considering his
options he smiled
at me

it said Rodolfo

Oh, Christ, I
thought
can't this guy

I said, "What does
your mother call
you?"

He said, "My mother
calls me *hijo*."

III

ARTS & SCIENCES

Xánath Caraza

MACUILXOCHITZIN

for Denise Low-Weso

Macuilxochitzin, I celebrate your poetry
You are an eagle warrior
From obscurity you come
Out of lost history, you emerge

"*A nonpehua noncuica*"
"I lift up my chants"
That phrase lives forever, Macuilxochitzin

You celebrate Axayacatl
The woman poet who records chronicles of war
"*In otepehue Axayaca nohuian*"
"Axayacatl conquered all places"

In your poetry you remember
The women who saved Tlilatl
The man who wounded Axayacatl

Macuilxochitzin, you have flowers in your blood
Your chants, your poetry
In Xóchitl in cuicatl
Are remembered forever

At forty-one years of age
You composed eternal words
All over the earth your chants leave their mark

Poetry claims you, Macuilxochitzin
Your nobility is reflected in your stanzas
Woman of jade words

Macuilxochitzin, poet with obsidian blood
Let the chants begin!
Let the dance start!
¡yn in cuicatl!
¡yn maconnetotilo!

Cindy Williams Gutiérrez

SOR JUANA ON IMMORTALITY

I, a mere woman, cloistered nun in a convent,
Dare to trifle with reason, even assert
Heresy on occasion. I fail to repent
And hide my inky scourges beneath a hair shirt.

If I must fall, let me pen my own dissent.
Let the splendid correspondence of stars subvert
Malefic orbits of those who mete my torment.
Let all my *loas* and *décimas* rise in concert.

And when at last I dream away from earth,
May there be no knell or *romances* of lament—
Only *villancicos* of birth and rebirth.

First, tear my scribbles into hosts of parchment
And dip them in my red signature not yet dry.
Then place each one in the open mouth of the sky.

Gail Tremblay

WATCHING THE OSAGE GODDESS

for Maria Tallchief

We sat in the dark hall in plush seats
watching you dance the Sugar Plum
Fairy in the Nutcracker Suite. You moved
and magic filled the room; grace
electrified the air that defined
the space you inhabited as arms
and legs stretched into shapes
so divine you were named America's
first Prima Ballerina. I was a soul
transfixed, a startled eleven-year-old,
barely aware a Russian genius was
so disarmed by your beauty, he created
these steps with you alone in mind.
The whole world desired to see you move,
and you obliged, whirling on point
and floating through the air, lifted
by a man who seemed to be there merely
to make you fly through space charged
with sparks reflected as light glanced
off your shimmering dress. My heart
beat quickly as my sweet, dark father
leaned over to whisper in my ear—
"See, American Indians can do anything,"
and I knew he meant for me to try.

Colleen J. McElroy

SPRUNG SONNET FOR DOROTHY DANDRIDGE

1922-1965

A woman unadorned stands out in a crowd of otherwise
Camouflaged women, and takes from her shelf all manner
Of potions and powers, the oils and slick pots of color
That hold electricity and confusion of mimicry
That test the ties that bind deception to reality
A woman in sundappled skin can mislead with mad
Profusion and tricks that others would give an eyetooth for
These are the women who would step away from themselves
Who know elaboration gives us our most handsome species
Who teach us disguised animals need not dissolve
Into surroundings when anonymity is not our destiny
Who know to understand the zebra's stripes, you must get down
    On your hands and knees where the vertical whites vanish
    Into the sky and the blacks take on a shape so indistinct
    The world's a blurred kaleidoscope of the mundane and bizarre

Where Whites say with black/ Blacks say black with white

Helen Rickerby

from ARTEMISIA GENTILESCHI, 1593 - CIRCA 1642

WOMAN PLAYING A LUTE, CIRCA 1610

She seems naïve to me now
holding the lute
across her body
as she looks
towards the sky
My father taught
me to paint
'You are very precocious'
he said, 'for a girl'
but he thought some extra
tuition in technique
would be beneficial
And Tassi certainly taught me
I learned my lesson well

SUSANNA AND THE ELDERS, 1610

Susanna is a serpentine S
as she twists away
from the gaze
from the faces of the
lechers, one old
one younger
They taunt her, they
whisper as they refuse
to share the paints, as they
leave her only the worst brushes
'Hey girl,' they say, 'I'd like
to get a lick of you'

'She can't be a virgin
just look at that mouth'
The other men, the judges
heard evidence that
indeed I was a virgin
until, by force
and I swore to it as they tightened
the thumbscrews
Tassi was out of jail
by the next time it rained

JUDITH SLAYING HOLOFERNES, 1612 - 1613

Your eye is drawn
to the place where their arms
all meet
Holofernes, the tyrant
lies back, tangled
in the sheet while
Judith, with calm
precision, slices off
his head
Abra, her maid, has the trace
of a smile
as she holds him down
The blood on the bedclothes
is the same colour
as Abra's dress
You may note
that Holofernes
bears a striking resemblance
to Tassi

SELF PORTRAIT AS THE ALLEGORY OF PAINTING, 1630

My shoulder
in my favourite green gown
protrudes from the picture plane
towards you
I am paused, caught
in the act of painting
I am both artist and model
both creator and muse
a perfect synthesis
Igegno—a genius light
strikes my forehead
My painterly arm
is strong

Lyn Coffin

from CAMILLE CLAUDEL

Welcome to Montdevergues, asylum
for the cold, the insane, and the inconvenient.
The first time I saw Rodin, I was hopelessly
young, and believed in the power of my
intelligence to save me. Rodin
said he'd devised a word test to see
if a young person like myself
had what he called "sculptural promise."
He asked me to say two nouns quickly,
without thinking. When I answered,
he gasped, and accepted me as his student.
He told me future sculptors favored
an abstract/human conjunction. I
had answered "Death" and "maiden." I asked,
"But which of the two is *human,* which
abstract?" When I was a student of
Rodin's, the *first* thing he made me abandon
was my insistence on authorship.
He'd have me model his draperies,
his legs, his penises—oh, yes,
nothing at all was sacred—Or, rather,
it was all sacred because it came
within our dedicated reach.
My specialty was hands . . . Rodin
and I both stood by a river, watching
an autumn leaf float by: but Auguste
tried to capture the leaf, to make it
stay, to turn it to a bead
of leafness in the mind. The leaf
was of no importance to me—except
as a way to understand the river.

I wanted to work obdurate stone
in such a way, it had no choice
but to exemplify the deepest
human dream—the dream of motion,
emotion, swelling to release!
No one but a fool would compare
my work and Rodin's, the work
I used to be allowed to do . . .

Darcy Cummings

PHOTOGRAPHING THE DEAD INFANT: INSTRUCTIONS FOR THE NEW EMPLOYEE

Once the request for services has been received,
proceed with all haste. Remember: time is of the essence.
Rent a horse or take a street car if the Company carriage
is not available. It is best to arrive promptly,
before the limbs have set. First, offer condolences
to the parents. Ask for a room with two facing
corner windows. If the attendants or family
have not done so, ask that the child be dressed
in its laying-out clothes. On a settee, table,
or couch placed between the windows (to take
advantage of natural light), place the child
on a pillow or blanket as if asleep. Ask
the attendants to leave (if rigor has set in,
it may be necessary to force the limbs
into a pleasing position). Since light in the eyes
fades almost immediately post mortem, close
and weight the eyelids with pennies. Support the jaw
(a table napkin can be folded and placed beneath the clothes).
Try to keep the lips in a natural line, slightly
open. Inserting a small piece of cotton wool
under the upper lip aids in the illusion of sleep.
Arrange clothing and hair. Set up the equipment
(see pamphlet three, "Portraits Taken in the Client's
Home"). Take several extra plates. Remember:
everything must be perfect. Ask if the parents wish to be
in a portrait with the child. Suggest the mother
sit in a chair holding the child; the father may
wish to stand beside them. Proceed as to
their wishes. Should the parents begin
to weep or cry out, discreetly withdraw.
Before you leave, again offer condolences

on the passing of their beautiful child.
In two weeks, write and ask when it would be
convenient to return with the portrait.

Jennifer Clement

WILLIAM HERSCHEL'S SISTER, CAROLINE, DISCOVERS EIGHT COMETS

In the Fahrenheit of my pulse

I feel their dust tails,
hear them rustle
in my fringed sleeves.
Shaped like F clefs,
rib-stitched,
I have found the new lights.

On cloud-white evenings
I draw fish hooks,
draw the eye, shank, gap,
throat, bend, barb, point
and polish the telescope,
rest my eyes. Wait.

Whatever
the sky gives me
I will take.

Jo Pitkin

BIRD, MOON, ENGINE

Like a fence or a wall to keep me from harm,
tutors circled me with logic, facts, theorems.
But I hid the weeds growing wild in my mind.

By age five, I could plot the arc of a rainbow.
I could explain *perpendicular* and *parallel*.
In my mind, I heard the wind in wild weeds.

Divided in two, my wiry system flew, flew.
I let those weeds wild in my mind unfold
as my unmet father's art seeped like rain.

Mother, Father, my mind finally loosed
its dark tangle of weeds. From drawings,
I milled notes lettered A to G for an unbuilt

machine that would compute loss and gain—
and reconciled my territorial heart, my brain.

Augusta Ada Byron King, Countess of Lovelace (1815–1852), was the daughter of British poet George Gordon, Lord Byron. A gifted mathematician, she wrote a set of complex instructions for Charles Babbage's proposed Analytical Machine, creating the world's first computer program.

Carole Oles

THE CHARLESTON ENTERPRISE
EXCLUSIVE ON MARIA, 1884

She was the woman predestined by Providence to show
the world that the American female mind is capable
of digesting mathematics in its entirety. It is true
some of them make crazy-quilts which is against the sex
intellectually; but one Maria Mitchell counts for more
than a million of these. She is our most distinguished living
astronomer of either sex. *She was predestined to show.*

Her hair is white but her black eyes sparkle with all
the fire of youth. Intellectual people never grow old.
To the best of everyone's knowledge, she has never in a single
instance refused to tell her age, which is the severest
possible test of intellectual strength in a woman.

The girl inherited her father's passion for mathematics.
She has his mind and brain over again.
Very early, when most girls are still in the candy-eating
and tear-shedding age, she became her father's assistant.
The one fact which brought her into fame was her discovery
of the great comet of 1847. She made a mathematical
calculation of its course and the paper is now in
the Smithsonian Institute. *She was the woman predestined.*

The girl astronomer lived a single life. In a confidential
moment one day she confessed that it was much harder
to keep girls from being married than to marry,
which is undoubtedly true. It requires far more heroism.

She has been working regularly on a salary 48 years,
without a break. Few persons, man or woman can
say as much. She began as Nantucket town librarian.

So small things lead to large. *She is our most distinguished,*
she was predestined, one Maria Mitchell counts for more.
The past 19 years she has been Professor at Vassar College.
Her heart is in her science and with her Vassar girls.
She says they have given her a nobler view of mankind.

Sarah Lindsay

RADIUM

His gifts to her were theory, patience,
equilibrium, and a pile of dirt—
industrial waste. He loved to watch his wife
aglow with determination, pursuing
discovery of a hidden element, past uranium,
by the light of her hunger. "I should
like it to have a beautiful color," he said.
He would buy her boots to wipe at the Sorbonne.

Heated, she leaned over a boiling vat,
stirring her dirt reduction, hour on hour.
She looked like any skinny hausfrau
bent to her bubbling sauerkraut.
She looked like the first woman who would be
awarded a Nobel Prize, as well as
the first to fall to her knees before
a hill of brown dust shot through with pine needles
and press her filled hands to her face.

She boiled her tons of pitchblende down
to a scraping of radium nearly the size
of their baby's smallest fingernail—just the white.
Proof of its existence, and hers.
It permeated their clothes, their papers,
peeled their fingers,
entered their marrow and slowly burned.
He mildly alluded to rheumatism.
He stroked her radioactive hair
with a radioactive hand.

Colorless, shining radium darkened
in contact with air. Chemically

much like calcium, it could stream
like calcium through her brain cellos
in her later years alone
and make memories glow in the dark:
illegal schooling, unheated rooms,
subsistence on tea and chocolate. Lying
with her husband for a few hours' sleep,
cracked hands and weakened legs entwined,
united gaze resting on the vial
of radium salts they kept beside them every night
for the lovely light it shed.

Kathleen Flenniken

SIREN RECOGNITION

Hanford, 1984

The orientation video begins with fire
and hurricane—familiar, comfortable disaster.
Then, with a queer segue, the *AWOOGA*
AWOOGA of commencing reactor meltdown.

I sit in my summer suit from Nordstrom,
the only new hire today, not dressed
for fear in the shape of a mushroom cloud
or the end of the human race.

The clerk sorts through papers as though
this is any work day. I believe in her
eye shadow, the orange on her desk,
but the siren sounds deep in my lizard brain,

in my involuntary heart which has
stopped and locked—the way security
(explains a calm voice in the video)
will lock down the gates and my chicken body

run in circles as my severed future fries.
Hear the siren once and it will change
your life. That night I'll wake transformed
into a cockroach, scaling the inside

of a reactor dome.

Martha Silano

PALE BLUE DOT

Candice Hansen-Koharcheck, I'm not sure how
to pronounce your name, but you were the first

to spot it, this two-pixel speck otherwise known
as planet Earth. Sitting at your screen, shades drawn,

office dark, you searched the digital photos sent back
by Voyager I, four billion miles from your desk.

And there it was, not the big blue marble swirling
with clouds and continents, not the one Apollo astronauts

the sheer beauty brought tears—thanking God and America,
declaring no need to fight over borders or oil; this was not

that view; this was how our planet might look to an alien.
And yet how close this photo came to not being taken at all—

scientists arguing aiming the camera back at the sun
might fry the lens, questioning the worth of such a risk,

this shot you say still gives you chills, dear Candice,
our planet bathed in the spacecraft's reflective light.

Pale blue dot lit by a glowing beam: I'm surprised
Christians didn't have a heyday, though viewing

His crowning achievement requires squinting.
When NASA put it on display at the Jet Propulsion Lab,

a blow-up print spanning fourteen feet, visitors touched
the pinprick so often the image needed constant replacing,

perhaps because without the little arrow we wouldn't know
which pinprick was home. And yet its barely-there-ness

doesn't excuse the plastic bags, duct tape, juice packs,
sweat pants that lodge in the stomachs of whales. And yet

its lack of distinction doesn't pardon the brown-pudding goop
on the Gulf of Mexico's floor, a goop in which nothing alive

has been found. To reckon that speck, mourn the loss
of the black torrent toad. To take it in, grasp its full weight,

then turn toward a child's insistent *give me a ride in a rocket ship!*
With meteors and turbulence! Like you, dear Candice, alone

and in the dark while a loved one's asking *Where are you going?*
When are you coming back?

*In 1990, Candice Hansen-Koharcheck, then scientist at the NASA Jet Propulsion Laboratory
in Pasadena, California, was searching through a database of images sent back by the Voyager 1
spacecraft. During her analysis she happened upon a tiny, two-pixel speck that turned out to be
a photograph of Earth. Today, Hansen-Koharcheck is HiRISE (High Resolution Imaging Science
Experiment) deputy principal investigator, which works with images sent back by MRO (Mars
Reconnaissance Orbiter).*

Mary Alexandra Agner

ORDINARY WOMEN SCIENTISTS

for R.C.

leave the lab late, flasks washed and waiting,
computer on an overnight crunch job,
warm dinner in the microwave
while wondering at excited water molecules,
wave their kids goodnight, grateful
to the man or nanny who nodded them off,
fall asleep to old friends' emails.
Ordinary women scientists love
the secrets of the ordinary world,
coax and capture them with math and models,
breastfeeding between the lines
of code and chalk notation on the blackboard.
Ordinary women scientists adore the limelight
ladies—Ros Franklin, Marie Curie, Liz Blackburn—
but they don't ache to *be* them.
Ordinary women scientists want an award
named after an ordinary woman scientist.
Ordinary women scientists make hypotheses,
they don't make the history books.
They make the scientific method sing.
Ordinary women scientists make change with every breath,
role modeling for the women in the lecture hall
front row, who notice how upright they stand
and how their stylish shoes eat up exhaustion.

Stacey K. Vargas

CIRCLE OF SILENCE

Like an electron trapped in an unstable orbit, I am seated in a circle
    of powerful men.
In an awkward moment small talk ends and the meeting abruptly begins.
The superintendent turns to me and says, "This was not sexual harassment."
I turn to the inspector general and say, "After everything you heard
    in this investigation, you find this acceptable?"
The inspector general turns to my department head but remains silent.
My department head turns to the chief of staff but remains silent.
The chief of staff turns to the superintendent but remains silent.
The superintendent turns to me and says, "This is my decision and it is final."
I turn to the inspector general and ask, "Don't you have anything to say?"
The inspector general turns to my department head but remains silent.
My department head turns to the chief of staff but remains silent.
The chief of staff turns to the superintendent but remains silent.
I am trapped in a cycle of muted men
Like an electron transitioning from its ground state to a higher energy level, I
    break away from the circle of silence.

Why can't they?

IV

CORPORATE IDENTITIES

Stefanie Freele

REMOVAL OF ONESELF FROM CORPORATE IDENTITY

With the jaw of a mountain goat, one of their many managers declares behind the block-wide walnut desk how dark chocolate is simply orgasmic. Knowing anything sexual could be deemed harassment, the women on the other side of the desk—which functions as a crevasse separating importance from employment—will titter, elbow, cross short-skirted legs. He has the kind of jaw that represents a full cooler of a man's beer or a bucket of flat white paint, something heavy, blockish, exaggerated, thrice-broken. It is not a handsome face, but the jaw of the corporation, held above the collar of the company, rising over the shoulders of the department, and jutting beyond the administrative assistants. Later, when he leaves for a meeting, his words will be repeated, as in, *You dear, are simply orgasmic.* The afternoon becomes one of unusual office-hilarity. The women will feign bliss while filling out memos, simulate rapture while filing forms, ooze in faux ecstasy while sipping their afternoon espressos. By the time he returns from his "meeting," which is most likely a nap or a shopping trip to Big 5, the women are spent, having climaxed all afternoon. They will be robotically typing, returning phone calls in patient yet weary voices, shoes off under the desk, toes idly touching each other. Jackets rest on the back of chairs away from softly stained armpits. The tray of cookies displays a halvsie, torn tinfoil and crumbs. The boss will have missed everything.

Victoria Chang

[THE BOSS RISES UP THE BOSS KEEPS HER JOB]

The boss rises up the boss keeps her job
                the boss is safe the workers are not
         the boss smiles the boss files the boss
                  throws pennies at the workers

the boss rises up higher and higher the boss's
              head is the balloon getting bigger
       and bigger it gets harder and harder to hold
              on the workers do good work

the boss goes higher towards god's work
             higher and higher she shakes
       her legs tries to shake the workers
             off little bugs with little bags

of personal belongings in plastic bins like the Bens
          and Tims and their friends we
      can be bosses too can hold the cross
            but there is a cost.

Barbara Drake

THE TYPIST

I made 87 ½ cents an hour typing,
when I was a college student.
I was a great typist.
My woman boss used a Stenorette,
a recording machine with a mic
and a foot pedal,
to dictate puny little messages
about things that needed doing.

After I typed a message perfectly,
she would read it over,
change a word or two,
and ask me to type it again.
While I typed, she'd grab her cigarettes,
go down to the coffee shop,
and drink coffee with the Director.
I could tell she thought he was cute,
but he was married.

I had a kind of scorn for her,
that she couldn't type her own messages,
that she couldn't get it right the first time,
that she did so little
and I was paid so little.

Lesléa Newman

ADJUSTMENT I—SHIFTING PILES

I place a pile of credits to my left
and a pile of debits to my right.
After I type the numbers from the debits
onto the credits
I pile the debits on top of the credits.
Then I pull the carbons from the credits
and separate the copies into piles.
I interfile the piles
and bring them over to the files
where I file the piles and pull the files
making a new file of piles.
Then I make files
for the pile that had no files
and put them into a new file pile.
I take the new file pile
down the aisle
over to the table where Mabel
makes labels for April to staple.
I take the new labeled stapled file pile
back down the aisle over to the file
to be interfiled with the pile of filed files.
After I file April's piles
I get new debits from Debby
and new credits from Kerry.
I carry Kerry's and Debby's debits
back to my desk
and place a pile of credits to my left
and a pile of debits to my right.
After I type the numbers from the debits
onto the credits
it's 10:00
and we have exactly fifteen minutes

to go down to the cafeteria
and drink coffee
or go out into the parking lot
and scream.

Cathy Park Hong

ENGINES WITHIN THE THRONE

We once worked as clerks
      scanning moth-balled pages
into the clouds, all memories
outsourced except the fuzzy
      childhood bits when

I was an undersized girl with a tic,
they numbed me with botox
      I was a skinsuit
of dumb expression, just fingerprints
over my shamed
      all I wanted was snow
to snuff the sun blades to shadow spokes,
muffle the drum of freeways, erase
      the old realism

but this smart snow erases
      nothing, seeps everywhere,
the search engine is inside us,
the world is our display

      and now every industry
has dumped whole cubicles, desktops,
fax machines into developing
      worlds where they stack
them as walls against

what disputed territory
      we asked the old spy who drank
with Russians to gather information
the old-fashioned way,

now we have snow sensors,
          so you can go spelunking
in anyone's mind,
let me borrow your child

thoughts, it's benign surveillance,
          I can burrow inside, find a cave
pool with rock-colored flounder,
and find you, half-transparent
with depression.

Jennifer Fandel

A POWERFUL POEM

Because you are such a pathetic wimp, this is the poem
that slobbers on you and beats you up even as you conceive it.
This is the poem written on work time when your boss reminds you
you don't have your priorities straight, when he says, "Hey, remember
who signs your paychecks," all debonair and smooth on the outside,
all prick and asshole on the inside. And while he wants you to say
"Not me, it's you, boss," you can't, because the poem's slobbering,
foaming at the mouth, baring sharp canines not typical to other poems,
a specialty in this one. And even as you write this poem, you can't help
imagining yourself whirling in the big chair, signing your name over and
over again because this poem has great hope for you, sometimes
dreaming you President of the United States, occasionally a taxidermist.

By writing this poem down, among all the poetry afloat in the world,
you've elevated its status, and by revising it and polishing it
(on work time you might add), it has taken on powers of its own,
has become a superhero of poems, is multiorgasmic, never tires, don't take
no shit from nobody, and though this poem has an obvious way with words
that you don't have, letting your boss bully you like that, mumbling
to your coffee mug that you ought to give him a piece of something,
this poem socks it to him loud and forceful, shaking its head, pointing its finger,
yelling, red faced, veins bulging, "I quit. And shove this job up your ascot."

And while you like seeing this poem do the work of a class bully,
ruthlessly demanding lunch money, whole wallets, people's tax rebates,
saying mean and true things to the elders, the higher-ups, the CEOs,
giving a little attitude a long way, this poem is deep down
a really good poem with good intentions who doesn't want to see
a good person like you be silent and afraid, who wants you
to stick up for yourself, you pathetic poetic pansy.

Cathleen Calbert

TEMP

Katie Gibbs is gone,
and all those cigarette-smoking,
sad-haired girls have vanished
into other kinds of cubbyholes.
I became something else and anyway never was
what I pretended to be. I thought: *This isn't me,*
isn't my life, this is barely even happening. Little did I know
this was as real as any other moment
and what I'd thought disguise was just shitty clothes:
plastic taupe heels and ink-stained purse,
poverty's version of dress-for-success.
That's what I got with my pretty good vocabulary
and my lousy phone skills
and my cute enough tuckus—which one, lunch-drunken boss
said he wouldn't let himself grasp. *Oh please,*
I thought and didn't think. *Do something,*
touch me, see me, let me slap your mustachioed face.
Bored out of my mind, I did all the non-jobs—
alphabetizing, typing labels, and licking
envelopes—before I limped off to a cheap lunch
below the Transamerica pyramid or whatever
other building Kelly Girl (really? seriously?)
had sent me to. On the street, I was young
but invisible, gazing at girls
who were young and rich, knowing
I was running out of time
to be both simultaneously,
and at the end of my 9 to 5 asking my mother,
How do you do it? She laughed, but I
didn't think I could do it. So I didn't.
That's why I have an easy life
I no longer like
but can't leave.

Sandy Shreve

OUR GIRL FRIDAY

Last week, every pencil I needed
sharpened at the feel of my reach,
paper clips untangled at my glance,
stacks of paper collated without one
licked finger;
a mere pat of my palm trained the stapler
to chatter perfect trilateral welds
into documents that distributed themselves
at the behest of my breath;
my fingers found required files
at the first touch,
labels emblazoned precise categories
onto folders in response to my very thoughts;
I had exact answers to everything
before I was asked.

Last week, efficiency was embodied in me.

But the people I work for
took all this for granted
and my paycheque remained the same.

So this week, I rewarded myself:
I exorcised the office
of its favourite possessive pronoun,
and announced *My Name*;
I vaporized the word girl
and pronounced *Woman*,
then I slipped my fingers into scissors
released Friday
and walked off with her.

Kate Rushin

UP FROM THE LADDER

Every morning I am sucked up,
pulled along by the subway,
like a bundle

in a pneumatic tube, then dropped
into this concrete, tinted-glass,
multi-million-dollar mausoleum.

It's dark when I leave in the morning;
it's dark when I go home.
But I'm grateful.

This building is mine, in a way.
I help to make it possible.
I fill not one, but two, affirmative slots:

My folks are proud of me, and the company
gets its government loan for cheap—
only 42 grand for the six of us.

My spunky, cheerful, boss is very
encouraging. She forever tells me
how bright I am. She marvels at my

ability to read and write on an
eighth-grade level, make simple decisions
without her. Ain't college amazin'?

Now don't get me wrong. I'm glad to get
this seven-thousand-before-taxes,
what with the riot money all dried up.

117

I rewrite convention announcements
for a hardware magazine while I binge
on honey buns and bad coffee.

Although I'm underneath the ladder,
I know they need me; I help to keep
this whole show running.

Rikki Santer

RE: SECRETARIES FROM HELL

We are typing typing typing smuggling our words onto the backs of your furthermores and enclosed-you-will-finds. We draw fangs on the happy faces of your Post-It notes, stir powdered laxatives into your coffee creamers, hurl executive bathroom keys through the air vents of your waiting rooms. We will blame visiting children.

Some of us drive black '69 VW vans and like to curb our rusted fenders into your corporate parking spaces. We wear sunglasses at our desks and make secret lists of Naugahyde jokes. Often, we snicker at your matching teak veneer while lodging mint toothpicks into their pressboard frames.

We know where everything is. We have lunch beers and greasy hamburgers at Bruno's Rainbow Tavern. At pinball machines we dangle cigarettes from our rapid fire lips. We read Kafka in dark booths or sit with the other gals and talk about YOU.

We listen to Metallica tapes through our Dictaphones while balancing your ledgers. We alphabetize third world dictators into your Rolodexes. We nickname you boss a nova.

We perfect photocopied images of our hangnails, butts and bunions then send them to your clients in their SASE's. We submit your home addresses to occult mailing houses. We add categories to your While-You-Were-Out messages:

—Sounded Canine
—Missing Brain Matter
—Out To Get You, Too.

Colleen Michaels

HAND TO MOUTH

The new girl who thinks she owns the tape dispenser is back again. Most fold after a week. Janet from shipping keeps a pool going. She gave this one three days. I saw her talking with the front office girls this morning, the ones who wear boot cut pants like my daughter does and keep hand cream on their desks. They say the carpet under their desks is filled with static electricity. Poor babies.

Everyone at the work table knows the tape dispenser is mine. I line the invitations faster than anyone. I can even work quickly with the slippery Mylar paper. I've got a system. I put the envelope down, flap up, give it three small pieces of double-stick tape, eyeball the liner, and lay it in neat and straight. If I were a cook, I could bone the shit out of a chicken. The guys in the press room call me "The Machine," and they send the biggest orders my way. I don't even need Band-Aids anymore.

Once I did the wedding invitations for Demi Moore and Emilio Estevez. Not many people remember that they were engaged. I keep waiting to see the invites show up on eBay, because I know we all snagged one to take home. Sometimes the guys who cut stock will pull aside extra for us. Right now we're working on getting the stock to put together Janet's grandson's first communion cards. We're a team like that.

The new girl keeps asking me annoying questions. "Where do you recommend for lunch?" I don't. Janet and I always bring pasta in Tupperware. Everyone knows that. "Do you think I should suggest handmade paper for a more dramatic effect?" No. I think she should just read what the P.O. says and start taping. And this one I just love, "Do you find the language on most wedding invitations to be more traditional or contemporary?" Do I find? I find that when I'm paid by the piece, I don't have time to think about questions. I wish she would just listen to her music with headphones like the other new girls who don't last.

Patricia Dubrava

THE END OF OFFICES (I)

On his way to a better job,
he was eager to unload this one:
shoved manuals into my arms, waved
carelessly over file drawers stuffed
with agendas and minutes—everything
I needed to know was there—
rushed me into meetings
I would staff next time.

City managers in well-tailored gray suits,
muted ties, spoke a language I barely knew, questioned
the absence of a jurisdictional issue. The man
on his way out had a glib reason for that,
added brightly, looking at me,
"She'll see it's on the agenda next month."
I was young and blonde and small and female,
made a note, felt their dubious eyes on me,
knew I had something to prove.

The fire chiefs, none under 50,
came to meetings in uniform, discussed
the fireproofing merits of various materials.
One white-haired chief scoffed, "You cook
your firefighters in those things."
He aimed his sights at me: "Don't suppose
you know anything about this, do you, young lady?"
his voice jovial with veiled bullying.
He shot the same question for each agenda bullet.

Finally, at the meeting's end, I summarized:
A: No, I don't know, but I'll research and get back to you;
B: We've agreed to schedule an expert briefing.

C: I believe we have a consensus
on the date, but I'm guessing, Chief X,
(looking at my tormenter wide-eyed)
you aren't happy with that either?
Bless them, the rest laughed loudly,
Chief X grinned and flushed and gave me
no more grief. The building officials, police chiefs,
and city managers took considerably more time.

Within a year, I'd expanded three of four programs,
and within two, put the one in the red
back in black. Three departments hired
their first female firefighters during my tenure.
When I fretted about hazing at one of them,
the chief's secretary snapped,
"She was in the Air Force Academy: she's been
hazed by a lot better than we've got."
And it was so. She handled them.
Chairmen of my committees came into my office
before their meetings asking, "What am I doing today?"
I'd tell them. In four years, I was Employee of the Year.
Only as I cleaned out files when I left,
two years later, did I discover that the young man
I replaced had started the job five steps higher
on the salary schedule.

Stephanie Barbé Hammer

MEMO TO THE FACTORY OF TEARS

for Valzhyna Mort

To: the Factory of Tears Collective
From: Management
Re: Benefits—fiscal, political, metaphysical and misc (i.e. Items not
  categorized under the forgoing Rubrics)

1. The Management has received your Requests.

2. Management met with the Board of Directors
In high-rise Buildings overlooking the Boulevards
Of Bonds, above the squalid Investments which Management
Avoids mostly through the use of special Elevators and
Limousines waiting outside a secret Exit at the Back, near the Garbage Cans.

3. We deliberated, which means talked. We had Luncheon
Sent in and then Dinner. We billed many Hours.

4. We have concluded the Following:
    4.a. the Answer is

No.

    4.b. A detailed Report of this No—its Whys, Wherefores, and Futures
(along with substantial
Graphs, Images, and Forecasts of why No matters and why No is right)
will be made available
In a few Months or Years.

    4.c. Employees may use their Security Clearance to access
The—

(Message truncated due to Size)

Ellen Mayock

WHAT THEY DO WITH COMPLAINERS

They like to remove thin-skinned plaintiffs,
you know, those complainers who just can't take it
the way they're supposed to.

They like that term, the thin-skinned plaintiff,
but I like to call us reasonable people,
think-skinned plaintiffs,
fair-minded plaintiffs,
strong,
sure,
unafraid,
outspoken,
ready.

What would a reasonable person do in this situation?
I think she damned well wouldn't take it
the way she's supposed to.

Not too long after I was offered the "opportunity to step down" from an administrative position in which I was harassed by my direct supervisor, I attended an informational meeting on Title IX that my university was offering. The room was packed, and I was seated in the back. Someone in the audience asked what happens to the complainant and respondent in a sexual harassment case once the case has been initiated. The general counsel's response was, "Well, we always try to remove the thin-skinned plaintiff." That's when I realized that my removal had been part of a greater strategy that was influenced by legal language and guided by the notion that the "complainer" is a greater danger than a harasser.

Dorothy Alexander

HONEST WORK

I never dreamed of becoming a high-rise, striped-tie
attorney-at-law. No. My dreams carried me back
to a place like my hometown. A version of Spoon River,
where I solved the problems of farmers, hairdressers,

waitresses, old women bamboozled by magazine salesmen,
harried housewives trying to escape drunken husbands,
their barroom brawls and relentless fathering of children.
A country lawyer, a latter-day female Atticus Finch.

I began by opening a practice in an old barber shop
on the main street of a ragged western town, leaving one
barber chair up front, visible from the street, bait for lanky
farmers and cowboys who favored this manly furniture.

Harley Russell, toothless, scabbed and calloused, was first
to come inside. He couldn't resist propping his manure-
stained boots on the footrest, pouring out stories like water
from an artesian well. Soon angle-parked trucks lined the block.

I tried to follow the advice of an old grizzled lawyer from the next
county who said, "Little lady, write as many $35.00 wills
as you can, take extra good care of yourself, outlive all of them,
then probate their estates. That's where the money is."

I drafted wills for relatives, neighbors, strangers who wandered
too near the old barber shop. I read abstracts of title, memorized
the Uniform Commercial Code, negotiated oil & gas leases, sued
magazine salesmen, kicked drunk husbands' asses onto the street.

I worked hard, did the best job I could, built trust, until
I was completely absolved of the sin of being female.

Marianne Szlyk

A PARALEGAL IN DC

I am allowed to wear red or white
but not orange or peach.
I am allowed to eat in the break room
but not at my desk.
I am not allowed to date
coworkers.

I have become translucent,
but I no longer need sunscreen.
Spring and summer are rumors
seen on a webcam.

Only the receptionist has flowers,
scentless orange and peach,
fresh, not silk.

Hands up my sleeves, I wonder
where all my time in this city has gone.

Meredith Quartermain

THE LAW LIBRARIAN

is new to the firm, taking over from Miss Spinks who died, and it is she who must stop the law books from disappearing forever in the lounges, board rooms, associate's offices, photocopy rooms, and lairs of the partners. Once a month you will please audit the library and retrieve all missing books, the managing partner and the chief accountant instruct her, in their dark blue suits and crisp silk ties (she wears straight black skirt, white blouse, sensible pumps). Nighttime while the partners wine and dine, she sets off with her wire trolley. In ancient Greece, she'd have cleaned stables of 3000 cattle or collected golden fleece from a herd of sun-crazed, furious sheep. Stockwell, Q.C. She unlocks the door. Here she might've fought three-headed dogs or a stygian sleep. But no, there they are—the missing *Criminal Law* by Fraudster and *Equity Law* by H.R.H. Oil. And here's another—how surprising to find it among Stockwell's hunting trophies and gun racks: *A History of the Common Law* by Joan Miró. She fingers its amazing maps of figures and lines. Begins writing a note to Stockwell: *Bravo! Bravo for choosing such a book.* A jingle sounds in the passage. She steps out on the patio, then climbs the rose trellis to the patio above. A man on his cell-phone: *No I don't want the property without the tenants, you keep bringing this up and I keep telling you.* The librarian slides open his patio door, his vast apartments open to other grander arrangements of couches, vases, fireplaces, gold, glass, silver, bronze, oak. At last she finds the entrance, with its double teak doors, which for her is an exit.

Kristen McHenry

PROBATIONARY PERIOD

They say there's cameras but they won't tell us where.
See, there's all these little games you have to play.
I can't explain, you have to just know them.
Lois was the gal before you. Just between us,

she was let go. We had to *let Lois go*, they said
all delicate, as if we didn't know a thing in this world.
As if we couldn't see for ourselves exactly what went on.
Well what happened was she just stopped wearing bras.

No one had the gall to say it to her face, but
everybody knew. Can you imagine, a gal that age,
flapping around with stretched-out cans showing
straight through her old-lady blouses. She went on that way

for weeks. Angie says it's 'cause she never did have kids.
It does something to a woman's head in old age,
according to Angie but of course Angie
wears crystals and reads cards in the lunchroom. Boss

ever found out about *that* there'd be hell, but
no one rats out Angie 'cause they're scared she might have powers.
You'll do alright here. You'll be okay.
Just watch for them cameras and keep in some decent brassieres.

Ann Cefola

FIRST JOB

The salesman cradles my foot in Italian kid. He doesn't know

I wash these stockings nightly,
    wear this B. Altman's suit three times a week,
        work for someone with short thumbs who panics easily,
            call secretaries in Paris who laugh at my French,
                have learned to say *Ne vous moquez pas de moi.*

In the soft peach light of the Saks Shoe Salon,
    he kneels and watches my face as I try spiked heels.
        I apologize, *My left foot feels crunched.*
            That, he says, *we can fix,* disappearing into the back,
                a man willing to stretch $100 leather for an undecided secretary.

Once again, I turn and walk, turn and walk,
    knowing my tender foot can never wear this point, this unsteady heel.
        He doesn't know I'm not here for a shoe that will fit.
            It's the quality of mercy at Saks I like.
                I don't lie when I tell him:
                    I'll think about it.

Susan Cormier

THREE KEYS

Years ago, my first real boss taught me two things. One: Listen to the boss. Two: Listen to your head and heart. In case of discrepancy, do what is right.

1. Today, my head aches with sandpaper smiles and the fumes of polyurethane shoes. Against my heart, the jangle of three keys on a lanyard. Check shoes right and left, same size; scan barcode; enter payment; bag purchase; smile; repeat.

2. My spine aches with double shifts and five-hour sleeps. While waiting for a credit card to ring through, I call my chiropractor's office.
"The number you have reached is no longer in service."
I leave a message on his cellphone. "Hello, this is Susan. I can't get through to you. I am worried. I need you."
Check shoes right left size barcode payment bag repeat.

3. As I hang up the phone, it rings. I juggle paperwork, small change, telephone. It's my boss, calling to tell me he's denying my request for a new ladder.
I remind him that already two of my salesgirls have been hurt from falling off the store's broken and wobbly ladder.
He tells me that obviously I need to train my staff on proper use of a ladder. And furthermore, if my part-timer refuses to use the vacuum cleaner because it spits smoke and smells like burning flesh, instead of a new vacuum cleaner I should get a new part-timer.

4. A little boy tugs on my pants leg. "Lady, how old are you?"
I tell him that today, I am really old.
He asks why I have green hair.
I tell him you are what you eat, and I eat a lot of broccoli.
Right left size barcode payment bag repeat.

5. I balance on a floor slippery with a layer of plastic shopping bags, dropped pennies, and till receipts as I headcount the lineup of customers and hand a lady her purchases. She clicks her tongue at my wrist braces and asks if I am working alone again.

6. Before I can answer, the phone rings.

It's my boss, wanting to know why I wasn't working yesterday.

I tell him it was my day off.

He says that is irrelevant; there is work to be done.

He says that contrary to my request, the store's carpet does not in fact need to be replaced.

After too many months of arguing, I am not concerned with watching my fucking language, so I remind him that my carpets are saturated with shit from a burst sewage pipe.

My customer looks horrified and scurries out the door.

Right left size barcode payment bag smile repeat.

7. Little boy asks how many earrings I have, and how I got them through my ears.

I tell him about a million, maybe more, and most of them were done with a big needle.

He looks impressed.

I tell him two of them were done with a gun.

He looks horrified.

8. A customer counts out pennies on my glass countertop. I pretend to watch, but really I am counting the reflections of burnt-out light bulbs and weighing the consequences of my bosses' wrath versus the logistics of climbing a broken ladder balanced on a shit-stained floor with both hands bandaged to change four damn light bulbs.

9. The phone rings. It's my boss. It sounds like I am wrong again. I say, "We appear to have a bad connection. I can't understand you," and hang up.

10. Little boy tugs on my pants leg and asks if I am really really old, or if I'm just pretending to be. He stands on his father's toes and says, "Daddy, hurry up. The store's closing and we're gonna get locked in. This isn't a good place to spend the night."

I do not tell him I know from experience he is right. I lean over and whisper, "There is always a way out. I have a magic key to the magic door."

He glares at me skeptically. There is no such thing as magic.

I pull my lanyard off over my head and hand it to him, keys jangling. "Have you ever seen a key like this one?"

He turns in a circle, counting keys, counting doors. One for the front door, one for the back. And one square and pockmarked, heavy and exotic, no door in sight.

Right left size barcode payment bag smile.

Wide-eyed, he returns my keys in solemn outstretched hands and whispers, "There really is a magic door."

11. The phone rings. "This is a message from Telus Mobility. The following voicemail message is undeliverable: 'Hello, this is Susan. I can't get through to you. I am worried. I need you.'"

12. I lock the door behind the last customer and wave through the glass. The phone is ringing.

13. One: Listen to the boss. Two: Listen to your head and heart.

14. My head is full of sandpaper smiles and the fumes of cheap shoes. Against my heart, three keys jangle: one for the front door, one for the back, one for the bank deposit box. Do what is right. There is always a way out.

Jennifer Dotson

SCENTSITIVE OR HOW TO BE A FRAGRANCE MODEL

The Agency has requirements.
I must be tall and slender.
I must wear high heels to
appear even taller.
I must keep my legs silky
smooth under my nylons.
I must wear a white blouse
and a slim-fitting black skirt.
I must wear cosmetics.
My props are a sample basket
and a glass phallus of
eau-de-parfum.
I must approach potential
customers and in turn
be approachable.
I must smile when I am
ignored by women who
think I'm a Barbie.
I must smile and listen to
men tell me about their
sports cars and careers.
I must gently return the
conversation to the product
which is desire, passion,
and seduction carefully
packaged and promoted
plus a gift with purchase
of an umbrella or tote bag.
I must be persuasive about
the notes of each fragrance
and speak knowledgeably
about layering techniques

to make the experience last.
The Agency has requirements
but the Agency doesn't care
that my feet in high heels
ache and swell
on the department store's
polished marble floors.
The Agency is unconcerned
that enveloped in a cloud of fragrance
my head throbs.
The Agency expects me to
follow instructions and
exceed expectations to boost sales
even though after a full eight-
hour shift with a 30-minute
break for lunch I still can't
afford to buy the thing I sell.
The Agency knows there
are plenty of others eager
to take my place.

Luci Tapahonso

HARD TO TAKE

Sometimes
this middle of the road business
is hard to take.

Last week in Gallup,
I was in line at Foodway
one check stand open and
a long line of Navajos waiting
        money and food stamps in hand
        waiting to buy food and pop.

My turn and I fumble
dropping the change
        Sorry, I say, sorry
        The cashier looks up smiling
        first smile in 20 minutes of Navajo customers
        Oh—that's okay. Are you Navajo?
        I swear, you don't have an accent at all!

        She's friendly too quick and I am uneasy.
        I say to the people behind me
        Ha'ʼat'ii sha'ni?
        Why is she saying that to me?
We laugh a little under our breaths
and with that
        I am another Navajo
        she doesn't greet or thank.

My change is dropped in front of me
        and we are not surprised by that.

Merle Norman offers a free make-up job
        just the thing for a new look
        I say to myself and stop in
        for an appointment.

For 15 minutes, I wait for a saleslady
then I ask for an appointment outright.
        Just a moment, she says,
        someone will be with you shortly.

I wait some more while the salesladies
        talk about a great hairdresser,
        General Hospital and Liz Taylor.

So I just leave, shortly is too long,
seeing as I'm the only customer in the place.

I guess I can do without a new look
but this kind of business
        sure gets hard to take.

Jan Beatty

STICKING IT TO THE MAN

Lateeka's working, my favorite teller—
she's got wild nail art & fire red/
feather extensions.
In line: young guy in hi-tops w/iPod,
black blazer girl on her lunch hour.
Lateeka & I always talk hair & makeup,
she's in school for accounting.
A guy with 20-inch arms in a Hines Ward jersey/
cut off at the sleeves,
a white-haired woman with
a cane & her daughter
—no suits.
Restaurant guy walks up to the window
with a bagful of receipts—
the blonde teller working the line
leaves her post & exits side-door,
so it's Lateeka & people
roll their eyes & grumble:
Oh great, now there's only one teller up there.
Steeler guy shakes his head:
Jesus Christ, do you believe this?
Daughter to mother:
Why don't you sit down?
Blazer girl turns:
I'm late for an appointment.
Steeler guy waves his massive arms wide
like he's going out for a pass:
Hey, I got an idea—
why don't we shut this shit down & open up a bank?
We turn to see his arms jabbing the air
like he's trying to grab it down—
his neck red with rage.

He barrels out the door & we bust into
laughing, the air full with mutiny:
I new spot open, we inch forward like
fat cattle, clutching our checks
a little less tightly.
We have won for the day,
we are sticking it to the man.

Laura Madeline Wiseman

YOGA INSTRUCTOR TRAINING

My trainer was a young woman—petite, blonde,
       her body supple and strong. She sat in half-lotus
            at the front of the room, miswrote my name
twice, and said, *The policy changed,* when I asked
       for my free yoga mat. She seemed to think
            I knew what to expect of the two-day
training. She told me to read certain pages
       in a manual and sign a liability waiver
            while I kneeled. All the walls had mirrors,
but one. The fourth was a two-way mirror into a class
       of spinners who glared at their reflection.
            The heat wasn't on. Almost all the time we sat
on the floor listening to pose instructions
       and were sometimes thrown candy if we agreed
            to demonstrate inside our winter coats.
Though her eyes flicked over us and she spoke,
       she never seemed to acknowledge us. In the room
            she walked on her toes and pointed
to a mirror where she'd taped posters, telling us
       to copy it down verbatim but never pausing
            to let us. She encouraged us to purchase—
at a discount—corporate clothes, DVDs, and CDs.
       She led us through classes from the manual,
            twice turning up the volume deafeningly high,
and made us practice sun salutations without stop
       to the song *It Feels Good* on repeat. She practiced
            hers alongside my mat to show me
the correct, faster speed. At the end of each day
       we were made to hold hands, stand together
            in a circle, and share. Some of the trainees
bounced like jack-in-the-boxes to speak first.

We were all cold. On the last day the trainer cried
                in the semi-dark of the circle, thanked us
and wished us well. Because the norm was set,
            we repeated some version of this and gathered
                        our stuff, leaving the fitness center for the cold.

Mary Ellen Talley

GHAZAL: UNBUCKLED SHOES

Her arthritic hip won't bend to reach unbuckled shoes
so she heads to work wearing black unbuckled shoes.

Her husband would grasp her foot to slide it inside
but can't breathe, bend down, reach her unbuckled shoes.

She leaves him with his oxygen hooked up at home—
screen door flapping breezes, like her unbuckled shoes.

Easy on the gas she drives small town streets where trees'
dry limbs reach out to sun like her unbuckled shoes.

Texas dawn, Cracker Barrel Restaurant, she clocks in,
drinks a coffee-cup breakfast in unbuckled shoes.

The custodian props his broom beside her chair,
stops rounds each day to buckle both unbuckled shoes.

They smile as stroller babies throw sandals across
the restaurant floor and parents chase unbuckled shoes.

At 70, she enjoys spending her store discount,
part-time cashier standing in her now buckled shoes.

This well-enough day at its end, she arrives home
with tired feet, now dreaming of unbuckled shoes.

Helena Minton

AT THE END OF THE DAY

> A lot of work is about waiting.
>
> —*Philip Levine*

Wait at the time clock to punch out
the minute hand to move to 5
each clutching a time card as we
wait to punch
wait for the customer to approach
take his forms
wait for coffee, lunch
two lengths of time
push me pull me
wait it out
point A to Point B
time strung
like a clothesline
work, home, time off
voice on the phone
what are your hours
not enough in the day
first floor clock
never agrees with the second floor
their minute hands argue, tiny swords
they never join in a synchronized swim
agree to disagree
unless someone grabs keys,
taps her wristwatch
as she watches a colleague
button his coat
pull on each boot
someone rattles the front door
too late

wait for the elevator
to rise at glacial pace
the doors to open close
timer out of sync
pitch dark on the walk
activate the alarm
slam it off try again
turn back to test the outer door is locked

V

WHY IT ALMOST NEVER ENDS

Kim Addonizio

DANCING

It's better than being a whore—
no one touches her.
She can't even see them,
dim faces behind glass.
She watches herself
in the mirrors,
thinks *I must be pretty.*
She's supposed to smile
all the time, but it's hard.
Relax and enjoy it,
Nicole tells her. Nicole's been there
a year. She has a snake
tattooed around her ankle.
short spiky hair she hides
under a wig,
a pierced nipple.
Rita asks if it hurt
and Nicole laughs.
You're lucky you look
so sweet, she says.
They don't want to hire
any more like me.
I'm sweet, Rita thinks,
sliding her hands down
her own hips, smiling
at nobody.

147

Shaindel Beers

WHY IT ALMOST NEVER ENDS WITH STRIPPING

You start out doing it for the bucks—
more than you'd ever imagined,
enough, at first, to make up for the rest
of the shit that comes along with the job—
the groping despite the "No Touching" sign,
the bastards who bring in straight girls to con-

vince them they're bi, the girls nervous and con-
tinuously fidgeting, while cash—
sweat-stained tens—shake in their hands, signaling
you over to dance while they imagine
themselves anywhere but there. "It's a job,"
you tell yourself, you'll just hold out the rest

of the summer. But you realize the rest
of the girls said the same thing, and they've con-
templated quitting for years, give blowjobs
in the back for fucking crazy money.
You don't want to be them but imagine
living the way they do, see them signing

five-figure checks on shopping sprees, signing
feature dancer contracts at clubs. You wrest
with the fact that girls who have the image
of putting out make ten times more. Buy con-
doms. Keep them on you just in case. The sugar's
pouring in—you're only giving handjobs.

You hear what you can make at outside jobs
doing bachelor parties, you're signing
on for three most weekends, making it
hand over fist, stripping at clubs the rest

of the week. The girl who dances as Con-
suela Cummings says she can imagine

you being "the next big thing. Imagine
your picture on boxes—Not just a job,
a career!" You read over the contract—
mark Xs for things you'll do, or not, sign
on the line—$5K if you check the rest—
anal, gangbang, scat bring in the greenbacks.

These days you don't read contracts, you just sign
to compete with the rest of the gravy-
starved girls who try to imagine it's just a job.

Penelope Scambly Schott

"AND HOW ARE YOU GENTLEMEN ON THIS FINE FALL EVENING?"

In the gas-lit parlor,
five young ladies on love seats,
satin evening dresses reflected
in gilt-framed mirrors.
A discreet bell:
Madam opens the paneled door.
Whiffs of cold creep from the hall
where two gentlemen
lift their hats,
unwind their knitted mufflers,
the neatly purled rows worked
by wife or fiancée.
Everyone smiles:
the two brunettes, the redhead,
even platinum Miss Lillie, tossing
her curls like a dare.
A genteel soirée:
nobody mentions money or sex.
But hips touch. A hand wanders.
Corks pop.
Just so much.
Even the most ardent gentleman
cannot perform impaired.
Time is money.
The fellows choose.
The banister up to the second floor
has been polished by sweaty hands.
Discreetly,
let us close
the upstairs bedroom doors.
The peephole looks in, not out.

Octavia McBride-Ahebee

AN OLD WORLD SEX WORKER'S WISH
FOR NEW WORLD PATRONS

I would love to meet you
with the sun standing guard at my back
with a belly rounded with food
with my ears emptied of the wailing accusations of my glue-sniffing children

I would love to mount you
against your will, but with your permission
in your own alley parroting the sounds of TB-fired chests
between the dissonance of malarial moans and birth calls
against the leanness of a stunted papaya tree
in a lot of sleeping jasmine and homeless lunatics
with hunger breathing through your pores
with the cries of your own children streaming through your penis

I would love to meet you, then . . .

VI

CONSCIOUSNESS RAISING

Deborah Woodard

HELLO AND GOODBYE, OR MRS. DIAL TONE

UPON THE RETIREMENT OF THE MARSHFIELD PHONE OPERATORS:
ELVA, DORIS, FRIEDA, CLARA, GRACE, LILLIA, AND RAYMOND, TOO!

This last Tuesday evening, in the church vestry, Mr. Raymond Houghton, operator, offered a few words, the occasion for a couple of deftly turned anecdotes. "I have served you for ten years," chimed in Mrs. Doris Houghton, chief operator, "until the recent conversion to dial." Her handkerchief was now in evidence. "And if you miss us, don't forget that we miss you."

"Like everyone else, we had our griefs, too, our joys and woes," said Mr. Houghton. "There were some nights when one or the other of us was up all night. Through it all, we enjoyed it and felt we knew you."

No one to tell us whether school's let out, or when is Mass. In their stead, Mrs. Dial Tone, a soulless robot hums, indifferent to our needs. Dial your party and the phone will ring, and that's the whole of it. Conjure in vain a dotted silk blouse with puffed sleeves. The sunny room is quiet, where Doris sat, her skillful fingers linking up our lives. No longer does Frieda trace our children, and call back.

Grace's words were simple. "Hurry, my dear," is what Florence heard. She filled in the rest: trains run today from Springfield, and tomorrow a general resumption of the strike. I am ready to orchestrate delirium against a dark-as-coffee sky.

Those days are gone forever. "Agnes, you sound as though you have a cold." "If my husband calls, I'm at the Grange, and home by 9. Our daughter's skillful fingers will give birth today (recital!)."

After the ladies were presented with corsages and Mr. Houghton with a boutonniere, the curtain was rung back, revealing the refreshment table. There followed a spirited skit, "The First Telephone," ably played with Mr. Robert Schwartz as Alexander Graham Bell, with Mary Beaton on accordion, rendering "My Wild Irish Rose."

Gifts of compact and silver were presented to the operators from the people of Marshfield. Mr. Houghton received a pen and pencil set. Florence Woodard recited her original tribute, "Hello and Goodbye," which was bound and printed for the honored guests. The cake, topped with an icing phone, was created by Mrs. Homer Darling of Cabot.

Mrs. Gosland was unable to be present due to illness.

Thank you, dear friends, for everything! Though we are scattered now, like beads that slide about the vestry floor, once strung by Grace (and Raymond, too), we remain bathed in sizzling purple light, the sheer delight of far-flung (and close-knit!) talk.

Marshfield, Vermont; March 19, 1957

This poem is based on a poem by my mother, Florence Woodard, who, before her marriage and subsequent move to Marshfield, Vermont, was a union organizer for AFL-CIO. Her poem celebrates telephone operators upon their "retirement": the party line had required live operators, but was replaced by dial telephones, so the operators (mostly women) were put out of work. The replacement of people by machines continues, and, in a gentle and affectionately eulogistic way, my mother anticipated it.

156

Susan Yuzna

THE TELEPHONIST

for David Foster

I had my order. Not of the choirs
of angels, but of the countries we called

in the stone dead heart of the night. Japan
was a young woman's voice, *a cool river*

through a thirsty land, sliding over my bone-
tired body like an icy, blue-green

wave. Australia was next—their perpetual
joking could keep me awake. I even

made history once: for eight years, a man
had been calling his brother in the bush.

He loved me, loved my voice, my flipping of
the switches in Oakland, California,

so that, at last, it worked. But usually
I was just too tired to care. My first

graveyard shift and I was much too tired
to give a shit when the businessmen yelled

about lines down in Manila again,
as if I could stop those typhoons, as if

I could make the old crones in Manila
love us, which they didn't, or be somewhat

helpful, which they weren't. *Why don't you try
again in two weeks?* I would say (the stock

response, a polite voice, then flip the switch,
cut him off, quick, before his swearing

poisons my ear). Too tired to care
about anything, not their business dealing,

not the drunken nostalgia for a whore
known during the war—he can't remember

her name, or the place where she worked, the street
it was on, but could I help him find her?

He's never forgotten . . . I grew so tired
of phones ringing for eight hours straight.

I wanted to pull my hair out, one thin
strand at a time. It was a newly

invented circle of hell, and if you
had been there, you just might understand

why that infamous *hippie girl* rose up,
out of her chair, yanked the earphones off, and climbed

onto a counter running the length of the room
beneath our long, black switchboard, then, crawling

from station to station, pulled each cord
from its black tunnel, breaking one connection

after another, like a series of
coitus interruptus all down the board,

before they stopped her, and led her away.
She must be on LSD, said a wife

from the Alameda military base. *And she wears
no underwear, either*, added another.

That was 1970, back when Oakland
Overseas was still manual, but the hatred

of a ringing phone is with me yet.
I will stand at the center of a room

and watch the damn thing ring its little head off,
and I will grin, quite stupidly, at its

helplessness. I will walk out the door, fill
my lungs with ice, head for the far-off peaks.

I will lose myself, become one small, dark stroke
in the white stillness of snow. I'm telling you

now, it was a brand new circle of hell,
but how could we know that, then? We had jobs,

the market was tight, and the union
won us cab rides home when we worked at night.

Sheila Black

"MY MISSION IS TO SURPRISE AND DELIGHT"

My daughter works in the Apple Store—the Help Center, open 24-7,
people from all fifty states, angry because their iPhones
malfunctioned or they don't know how to program their data
plans. She practices sounding knowledgeable yet ditzy; mysterious
yet lucid, and able to reassure. She has never been ranked down for
a "bad conversation," and they rate every call. Some of the kids
lose it—the ones who get fired. A bit better than minimum wage,
but not much. "You get addicted to the notion-what would it
mean to be the perfect Apple helper every time?" They reward her
with T-shirts. "You are the Future!" in a pretty Apple box. And
letters signed "Apple." "We know you have dreams. We know
you are the one we have been waiting for." They have taken
over the Wells Fargo Bank building downtown, a row of white
Apple cubicles made of slick plastic—beautifully designed. Steve
Jobs said "simplicity takes effort." He said "Apple is for the
person with the unique mind." After work, my daughter and her
co-workers bend over their iPhones. When I say "rosemary,"
my daughter Googles a picture of it. Her latest t-shirt bears the slogan
"My mission is to surprise and delight." This annoys her faintly.
"How can I wear it outside the Apple Help Center?" she asks. "Apple
loves you," says the latest letter. I want to say "You, Steve Jobs, did
not invent a machine alone. No you, Steve Jobs, invented a new
form of loneliness. No wonder you were not able to live forever.
The body has to get its own back somehow. How you have separated
each from each, self from self, the anti-parable in which
all breads and loves become as one. The silver apple, which
will never be edible, will never be baked into any kind of pie."
I ask my daughter how she does it—eight hours, call after call,
and everyone angry, or sad, or simply frustrated. "I never speak
as myself," she replies, "but as Phone Girl. Phone Girl has no
past, no present, no family. Phone girl is all light and longing.
She is only a voice, and a voice can be anything." My daughter
holds out her hands, "She is a light you can see straight through."

Ellen Bass

PHONE THERAPY

I was relief, once, for a doctor on vacation
and got a call from a man on a window sill.
This was New York, a dozen stories up.
He was going to kill himself, he said.
I said everything I could think of.
And when nothing worked, when the guy
was still determined to slide out that window
and smash his delicate skull
on the indifferent sidewalk, "Do you think,"
I asked, "you could just postpone it
until Monday, when Dr. Lewis gets back?"

The cord that connected us—strung
under the dirty streets, the pizza parlors, taxis,
women in sneakers carrying their high heels,
drunks lying in piss—that thick coiled wire
waited for the waves of sound.

In the silence I could feel the air slip
in and out of his lungs and the moment
when the motion reversed, like a goldfish
making the turn at the glass end of its tank.
I matched my breath to his, slid
into the water and swam with him.
"Okay," he agreed.

Laura Ruth Loomis

SOCIAL WORKAHOLIC

I write reports while talking on the phone
About a different case. This evening, I'm
About to take my files and notebook home.
A mother wants to talk. I don't have time.
I mix up names. Now they're all named "caseload."
Home visits every month? Girl, that's a joke!
Just tell the kids to line up by the road
And wave as I drive by, pretend we spoke.
My car, my office: which place do I live?
A lawyer wails, "She doesn't have a beeper?"
Between the foster parents, relatives,
Parents and kids, I'm everybody's keeper.

Biology's what finally protects us.
Thank heaven I was not born ambidextrous.

Willa Schneberg

INTO THE SOCIAL WORKER'S OFFICE
WALKS VIETNAM'S LEGACY

Portland, Oregon, 1997

With an uncomfortable giggle she says she picked me because she
read that ethnic minorities and sexual abuse were two of my specialties
and that she fit both categories. Her mother was from Dalat, and met her
GI father in a bar during the war. When her father was zonked-out on
crystal meth, a drug he first procured in Nam, she had awakened to find
him on top of her in their camper. There were always empty beer bottles
spilling out of cabinets. She doesn't remember when her parents
weren't drinking, but her mother did all the smacking, grabbing,
slamming and hurling. The round glass bowl filled with water and her
fish the color of the rainbow in gasoline, left a scar below her eye. Her
mother swept the dying fish into the trash. *Aren't I crazy calling my
parents every week when they never call me?* While she is still young
and sexy she finds a way to make her own money. She buys big bouncy
breasts. *Men are stupid and lazy.* She is sure she has more repeat customers
than the other girls behind the glass booths also touching themselves,
because they let drugs ravage their looks, while she ended her orgy with coke
six months ago. *Why do I always pick the ugliest boyfriends? I know,
because they won't leave me.* She talks about having no women friends,
but is scared to contact her best friend in high school, a Mormon, because
she wouldn't understand her lifestyle. *I loved going to her house. They all
sat down together and put cloth napkins on their laps.* When she tried
community college she did well, and can balance a checkbook just like
her mother. *I want to get out of the life, but I can't give up the money.
Do you think you can help me?*

163

Cortney Davis

HOOKED UP

Drunk, partying, she
and the man just *hooked up*
she tells me, the college student, the nervous
can't-sit-still woman,
dark-haired, laughing, pierced tongue,
pierced navel, colored threads
braided into bracelets around her wrist,
barely making it through finals,
graduating next spring then
maybe a Master's, but for today,
she says, the problem is fear,
What if I caught something, this worry
hooked into her and now
she slides down, eager but not eager
for me to do cultures, blood tests,
to tell her *everything is fine.*
Oh how often I've seen this,
this fear twisted in as if there might
really be a tangle inside, shiny, metallic,
like wire, and how each time
I have to pull it out,
strand by strand,
trying not to weep over this
one more woman *hooked up*,
these barbs deep into flesh,
and how they can only be extracted
with moans and cries, each one
ripping through until
there is only this woman and me,
helpless to do anything
but go on pulling the hooks from her,
stuffing them into the garbage,

telling her how sweet they must have seemed
that night, how she must learn to recognize them
before they gain entrance; how strong
she must be now, how resolute.

Miranda Pearson

WINTER (I)

It's winter, and the radiators gurgle and scald.
The nurses are getting tired
of the low pay, the skivvy work.
The prospect of working over Christmas again,
changing diapers while the manager
reads *The Sun* and smokes in the office,
his size twelves up on the desk.

You buzz into the locked ward,
meet the wall of warm air, the eye-sting
of stale urine. Shrug on your white coat,
pull on the powdery second skin of
plastic gloves (keep a spare pair in yr. pocket).

Lug sacks of wet and muddied laundry—
these are the facts of life.
Sit in the dark with a dying man as he
hallucinates crashing fighter planes,
as he shouts out to his co-pilot.

Tie bibs, spoon the soft food.
Carefully wipe the shivering bird-mouths.
Lift the white, onion-skinned hand
of a woman as she repeats her dead sister's name.
Do not yourself have a name.

The patients are drugged to a stupor
and the nurses also drink; a skyline of bottles
under the desk "for Christmas,"
dark rum and Bacardi—sticky stuff,
like medicine.

After the shift, meet the others
for a drink at the Staff Social, pint after pint of lager
till our faces rust and words slur.
Holding each other up, we weave and skate
along the sweeping driveway
to the gates.

Janice N. Harrington

PIETÀ

She stoops, this should-have-retired
aide, in her polished and re-polished
shoes and white uniform, lifting
this fetaled shape, the body
of a wordless man who only groans,
his eyes startled into clear ice.

His blue-milk skin, blue-veined
and blue-bruised, eases against her chest.
His brow leans into her shoulder. His lips
press her uniform's rough pleats and leave

damp wings traced in spittle above her breast,
though she does not notice and, straining,
bears the weight as the years have taught,
her knees bent, back levered into straightness,
breathing in, breathing out, muscles tight.
She lowers him as you would lower an over-
filled basin, settling its shallow wash gently,
leaving even the refracted light undisturbed.

Leah Zazulyer

MY MOTHER WORKS

in a nursing home
pushing wheelchairs
patting hands
carrying trays and
watching at the front desk.

One woman cries
and mother talks to her
as much as she can.

In recreation therapy
she leads the dancing
and sometimes sings.

She works so hard
and walks so much
that at night
they don't confine her.

Laura Shovan

THE MAMMOGRAPHER

A few years at this machine and I
forgot the breast itself, knew only
what low energy X-rays showed:
the hazy map of ducts I passed
to someone else, a fortune teller of sorts
who saw things in the mist—
a ghost congealing in that mass
of cloud.
       I groan inside
to see another blue gown open,
breast resting passive above the ribs.
(What microcalcifications are hidden
inside?) My job would have been
easier had God thought: muscle,
ligaments.
       Days come
when I am undone by tenderness.
I lift a breast, skin thin as a fontanel,
guide it to the camera's view. It's like
taking the arm of someone small or frail.
Sometimes, cupping a stranger's breast,
I imagine my hand slipping under
the head of a child I love, who has already
fallen asleep.

Belle Waring

THE FORGERY

—For uncrossmatched blood, the doctor must sign.

I said, It's for a baby! Stabbed in utero! *I'll* sign for the doctor.

—You mean *forge* it? Forget it.

The woman behind the blood bank counter then tapped on the page with her index finger, with her salon-painted nail, tuff as an escutcheon—tiny gold griffin on a field of carmine. O she had a haughty eye.

—*Physician's* signature, she said.

—Where's your supervisor?

—I *am* the supervisor. And I'm not losing my job 'cause a *you.*

And since no pity could move her, nor rank, nor threat, and a legal signature meant lost minutes, and since the baby was preemie, the baby was shocky, and it was four in the morning, gall of the night, I saw fit to go crazy.

—*Lose your job? Who'd want it?* I got two babies up there on *vents* already, and now *this* one, *surprise!* The mother walks into the ER, collapses, with multiple stab wounds, belly fulla blood, but when they take her to the OR and open her up *there's this twenty-eight-week fetus inside.* So they STAT-page us and the shit hits— OK? But you know why I like it? You get an admission, that crazy first hour, everybody works together, everybody helps you out, and you reach a point—not out of the woods, but you're getting there, *you feel it*— and somebody cracks a joke. You look up—you all laugh. That moment. *Help me,* I said.

She turned her back. Walked away. On the wall someone had stuck a poster:

IT HAS COME TO THE ATTENTION OF THE MANAGEMENT THAT EMPLOYEES EXPIRING ON THE JOB ARE FAILING TO FALL DOWN. ANYONE WHO REMAINS DEAD IN AN UPRIGHT POSITION WILL BE DROPPED FROM THE PAYROLL.

Then she was back. Plunked down two pints of blood.

—Sign, she said.

So I signed, I forged, I grabbed the two units, uncrossmatched blood, color of garnets, color of beets, hugged the blood to my chest and I ran all three flights and I ran, never tired, the talker, the forger, I ran with the gorgeous, ran with the anonymous, ran with the cold dark blood.

Sarah Zale

from "MADRONE"

V.

In the summer of '67, Detroit burned.
As the earth fell away, leaving roots naked
and shameless, I worked as a nurse's aide at Grace.
Smoke drifted from downtown, crossing words
etched in concrete above the hospital entrance.
Each day, there on the steps, I stood squint-eyed,
the stretch of my neck taut, my jaw loose and smoke
burning in my throat. I read: *God, grant us grace
to accept*—I wondered what it meant—
the courage to change what can be changed.

VI.

The other aides were of skin russet to black.
I watched them in a way whites know
about watching without seeing. As I folded
hospital corners, I gazed out a window,
eyed the white seeds of the dandelion blow.

VII.

On breaks I sat among them, not at ease enough
to be one of them, my laugh not free enough,
my voice a drive across Iowa—theirs
a saucy strut down Bourbon St.

I longed to go home with Hattie or Essie
or Mae, sit at her table, eat wild things: chitlins
and hog maws, red beans and greens. We'd drink
dandelion blossom wine and toast the tree
I didn't know grew on my street. We'd laugh,
sassy and free, because laughter tastes
so damned good.

Mia Leonin

NURSE'S EPITAPH

> Soft nurse of dear Idea, near me stay.
>
> —*Ann Yearsley, "Absence"*

She's a diabetic who craves strong sugary drinks—
a gaggle of maraschino cherries bobbing
to the surface of a tequila sunrise.

She once placed a small square transistor radio
in the crib of a thalidomide baby. Mongo Santamaría's congas

crackled on the moist pad and through the metal bars—
nose hole, eye pit, tuft of hair pulsed in perfect rhythm.

Kneeling among the orange vinyl bean bags, she poured
cans of vanilla Ensure into the stomach tubes of hydrocephalics—
frail bodies tethered to helium-blown skulls.

On weekends, she brought home crippled toddlers and Down syndrome
kids with names like Cowboy and Jodie.

She once saved a dog's life with the Heimlich maneuver.
The chicken bone shot across the room and dented a metal cabinet.

All those children and dogs are dead now.
My mother's slippers shuffle across the tiles of my house.

Camille T. Dungy

7 PROBLEMS IN PEDAGOGY

Because she must test them, because she has
turned her back on them, because they are trying,
because every eye is on her because the chalk's yellow rain
that has ruined all blouses has ruined this blouse
as well, because they will repeat what she tells them,
because they will do as she says, she writes
it all down on the board so they will remember.

•

When the winds warm and they bluster, each spring,
take us outside, take us, please, take us outside, she doesn't
admit, *I can't or I will lose you.* She tells them
what her teacher told her about his teacher
who gave in to such longing. Who taught class
outside. Already they are lost to the lesson she planned

•

First there are three. Take away one and what do you have?
My family. They understand subtraction. Try addition.
They surprise with their skills. Subtleties of language arts
are well under their command. One child raises his hand.
A question. Another demonstrates the exclamation, *He just peed!*

•

and she must return to the basics: green (grass), blue
(sky), yellow (rays of dandelion florets)—memory is built
by association, repetition, predictability, and fear—a dog
(red), the ring of students (circle), the teacher (square). She tells them

・

Because her father worked nights, because he told her to do something
with that brain of hers, because she needs to help others,
because they are waiting to learn what she knows, she tests them.

・

the story. The students laughed when the dog circled, sniffed the mark
(What is this? A plot. They should be able to recognize that.)

・

so like a tree, the sap, that teacher. Bark, dripping. The teacher kept teaching.

Sarah Brown Weitzman

SUBSTITUTING

Nobody likes a substitute
anything. It's the real thing
everyone wants.
So to survive
as a substitute teacher
just don't admit it.
Tell the kids
their teacher's not absent
just late
and will be arriving
ANY MINUTE.
In the meantime, pass out
an attendance sheet.
But when you read out the names
be suspicious and even skip
any with nicknames or
too many initials.
R.U. Cerious, Bill Bord,
Graham Kraquer and Jim Naceum
will convulse the class.

If you must turn
your back, simply ignore
the waves of obscenities,
comments on your figure
or its lack
moans and groans
sounds of gagging
and retching
and the class ventriloquist.
But unappoint at once
the class secretary

who writes on the board
so the chalk squeaks and screeches
and everybody screams
and shudders and writhes
in their seats
and even your skin crawls.

Send the kid who insists
the top of his desk
is really a bongo drum
with a note to a teacher,
say, a Miss Walker
stressing its importance
is the reason
you have for choosing HIM
to deliver this missive.
Tell him to search for her
EVERYWHERE.
DOWN in the office on One
UP in the cafeteria on Five
DOWN in the supply room
in the basement.
It will take him at least
two periods, hopefully
three, before he finds out
she's absent today.

If you must make threats
make them
vague and incomplete
and use BIG words like:
"If you don't stop running
around this room and
screaming, I'm going to
insist on pandemonium
in here and execute pirouettes."

Or: "The next one who gives me
déjà vu will be sent
to a strict monogamy."
If any intrepid kid
asks for a definition
just look fierce and say:
"You better hope
you never find out."

At the end of the day
if you make it through
and the dismissal gong
finally sounds
be sure you're not standing
in their path to the door.
And if the kids say
over their shoulder:
"It was great having you, Teach.
Can we plan on your coming back
tomorrow?" Say NO.
Kids love a surprise
but you won't.

Laura Da'

PASSIVE VOICE

I use a trick to teach students
how to avoid passive voice.

Circle the verbs.
Imagine inserting "by zombies"
after each one.

Have the words been claimed
by the flesh-hungry undead?
If so, passive voice.

I wonder if these
sixth graders will recollect,
on summer vacation,
as they stretch their legs
on the way home
from Yellowstone or Yosemite
and the byway's historical marker
beckons them to the
site of an Indian village—

Where *trouble was brewing.*
Where, *after further hostilities, the army was directed to enter.*
Where *the village was razed after the skirmish occurred.*
Where *most were women and children.*

Riveted bramble of passive verbs
etched in wood—
stripped hands
breaking up from the dry ground
to pinch the meat
of their young red tongues.

Kathleen McClung

NIGHT SCHOOL FINAL

You murmur, chew nails, joke, prepare to write
in ways unique to each. Semesters end
by rote: I stroll the narrow paths, dusk blurs to night,
I hand you tests like maps, a hush, then pens
begin to dig, carve bark, or sprinkle slow
faint wisps of sentences. Some know, some guess

and I refrain from staring, as I guess
you want trust, not suspicion, as you write.
My gaze brushes each forehead, tender, slow,
almost a mother's gaze as this term ends,
and change knocks, quiet, urgent, at a door. Open
and go, but first show mastery tonight.

What must your labor prove to me? Two nights
a week we talk of poems, soliloquies. We guess
together, muse aloud, stake claims. *Your pens,*
I say, *the tools of Donne, of Rich, to write*
mind body heart. Two-hour exam at end
may sift who's read from those who've not, but slow

absorbing, deepening require long, slow
inquiry, lasting years beyond this night.
We don't have years, we're temporary, end
with stapler, backpacks slung, a wave. You guess
I will be fair with letter grades. You're right.
Old-school examiner, my aim: sharpen

vision, equip minds for dilemmas pens
have not yet shaped for study, honor slow
approaches (plural)—not texting!—to write
what matters most. You twenty-three scatter tonight;

181

we will not meet again. Oh, sure, when I'm a guest
at bistros, Arcos, Supercuts, our chat will end,

perhaps, this way: *I learned a lot.* There is no end
for learning, we'll agree. I glance at pens
and faces now—full concentration, yes—
this room almost a home, almost dear. Slow,
the speed of cypress, chanterelles, this night
of harvesting mindfruit, this fertile rite.

My pen will forage slowly late tonight
among the guesses, fresh and wild, you write,
a tribe of thinkers in a forest without end.

Wendy Barker

ENDING THE SEMESTER IN AM LIT

The guy who served as a lighthouse
      when discussions had grown so foggy I couldn't
           steer us back on course, the one who never missed
a class, who camped in my office every
      Wednesday afternoon obsessed with Bartleby and
           Ahab, who made all As and wrote a dynamite final,
still hasn't turned in his long essay. Is he
      bleeding on a gurney in the ER, or moaning
           by the freeway in a pile of smashed glass and mangled
chrome? I e-mail, and he shoots back, "I haven't
      written it." No apology, no excuse. I offer an
           extra day. No response, not even to say he prefers
not to. I want to harpoon that essay and
      splatter it onto my desk. I give him till
           midnight, remind him, bold font on the syllabus:
"No essay, no passing grade." Still silence,
      nada, no paper. Where *is* that essay? I feel
           like Herman's wife Lizzie, nagging him, or Carlyle
insisting, "Produce! Produce!" Melville's
      narrator at least learned about his clerk's past
           at the Dead Letter Office, but I have no idea where
this guy works, or if he does. Is he playing
      some kind of game, resisting like Bartleby,
           forcing me to play Ahab, hunt him down? Why
can't I just give him an F? I've become
      the narrator in HM's story, his whole career
           questioned by the scrivener's refusals. Maybe I'm
remembering my own years as a student
      when I skimped time with my son to write
           all those essays, the dread dissertation, and then, later,
meet deadlines for grades, committee
      reports. Updating the CV to show every
           minuscule pebble I cast into the scholarly sea. All those

sleepy post-Christmas days I missed—leaving
          my boy and his dad in their jammies—to join
                    the tangled academic throngs at the MLA. On this guy's
final exam, he added a note that said
          our class changed him, he'd been on course
                    to become like Ahab, netting every A in sight, but after
finishing *Moby Dick* and then reading
          Whitman, he decided to spend more time with
                    his daughter who's just learning to walk, and he didn't
 want to miss a single one of her
          wobbling steps. He felt the pull to "loafe
                    and invite" his soul. But I'm left here anchorless,
like Melville's ship the *Rachel*
          searching after her missing sailors, her lost children.

Rhonda Pettit

ASSESSADEMIA

I.

Now I must teach by the grid,
wasting fuel to make thin heat, weak light.

Now I must generate goals and objectives
instead of jack-in-the-pulpits, jack-in-the-boxes, jacks of all trades.

Now I must prove my abilities
the way one might paint Picassos by numbers.

Now I must reach a bottom line
because what's at the bottom serves the top.

II.

Now I must market my courses to convenience,
my thinking to efficiency, my sense to dollars.

Now I must conceptualize a pedagogy—crinkum-crankum—
and practice professing it works.

Now I must remember that diversity is beautiful
and wonder where it has gone.

Now I must take a pay cut to pay for
the espresso machine in the recently refurbished administration complex.

Now I must watch the grounds of the Corporate University
brew into a bitter cup of *Gotcha by the tits!*

III.

Now I must say hello to the blossoming technologies
and goodbye to the wilting post-human humanities.

Now I must entertain through a screen
because students must learn to buy more machines.

Now I must teach to images of distant bodies
that are not stars or planets or moons or flesh.

Now I must always be online instead of writing lines.
We are programmed to retrieve.

IV.

Now I must teach a text instead of a tale, a process instead of a poem,
and forget that the best stories rise from blood and nerve and tactile generosity.

Now I must teach critical thinking
but not criticize the New American Nightmare.

Now I must teach my students:
Beware of your toys.

Now I must learn my not-so-new names:
Crank, Curmudgeon, Luddite, The Mad Professor.

Now I must somehow find in this job
the good work that answers despair.

Mary Makofske

HIGHER EDUCATION, 1970

My Shakespeare professor told the class
how she discovered her estimated worth.
Waiting in the office for her paycheck,
she leaned on the counter next to a colleague.
She had a car payment due, was calculating
whether she'd have enough for that trip to London.
When the clerk handed over his check,
her colleague laid it down and she saw the figure.
They taught in the same department, held PhDs,
had come the same year from prestigious schools.
Same title, same step, same glowing evaluations.
And his pay was more than hers. He was tall
and she was short. He was brown-haired,
slightly balding. She was blond, close-cropped.
She was single, he was married. He was male
and she was female. She saw which of these
factors figured in their accounting.

Bonnie J. Morris

WOMEN'S STUDIES PROFESSORS GET NO RESPECT

Women's Studies? You still teach that? Isn't everything, like, equal now?
How come there's no Men's Studies? Isn't that discrimination?
I'd like to see everything Human Studies, and eliminate women's studies altogether.
Do we even need women's history in 2012?
Hey, is this where all the feminazis hang out?

Our lives are still unspeakable
Our herstory still scary
Plunged in tepid waters of diversity

The first who taught this subject has retired
And feminism slowly packs its house,
Now boxed up, holy

The language of naming now a dialect
The spoken words of womanhood soon lost.

These days I'm feeling shelfish.
Not *shellfish,* like the oyster and the crab
Just dangerously close to being shelved;

As if the women's movement were a book,
(and going out of print)
and who reads those?

Shelfish, because I prowl for double X
On every bookshelf speaking to my sex.

The ones who came before we still ignore,
Or name as strident figures (and abhor)
Unknown as those who opened up the door.

I'm underpaid. I'm adjunct. I exist
To raise my writing hand up in a fist
So all our herstory won't fade in the mist.

Sharon Cumberland

KYRIE PANTOKRATOR

The world was not for me, but for my brothers,
the horses, the science kits, the classrooms,
the rough training for the world, which was not
for me, but for my husbands, the work, the money,
the camaraderie over drinks and waitresses, which
was not for me but for my fathers, the wives, the tidy
homes and waiting children, the warm bed,
which was not for me.
        I beat the chest of my soul.

The clear path was not for me but for the scions,
the boys of promise and grace, their football fields,
the locker room and all its promises, which was not
for me but for the scholars, their tutors, the books
and allowances, the mighty potential, which
was not for me but for the junior partners,
their swaddles of opportunity, the slap on the back,
which was not for me.
        I bite the tongue of my mind.

The audience was not for me but for the speakers,
their podiums and printing presses, the bull horns which
were not for me but for the soldiers, their flags and taxes,
the guns and petroleum, their certainty of righteousness
which was not for me but for the kings, the popes, the presidents,
their parades and treasure, their chest of ribbons,
which was not for me.
        I brandish the fist of my bowels.

The Church was not for me but for the Adams,
the ones who look like You in their secret bodies,
like the Father and the suffering Son in his ribs

and rags, which were not for me but for the saints,
their faith and miracles. Only the martyrs,
their persecutions, their resistance, the hopes
of forgiveness for their jealousy, their cowardice,
their despair, Pantokrator, are for me.
      I bend the knee of my heart.

Deborah Majors

WHO SAID WOMEN CAN'T PREACH?

Men try to tell me I'm the wrong sex
to stand behind a pastor's pulpit to teach and preach.
Vessels with womanly parts
can't be used by God to speak words spoken long ago.
Feminine lips can't repeat to men the letters of Paul for instruction
or the love song of Solomon for contemplation.
Tired little men with sweaty foreheads,
fat men with chinny-chin chins,
skinny men with veiny necks and boney fingers pointing,
say women belong in the pews for spiritual news.
Only men can lead from the pulpits.
It's God's way.

My reply is always the same,
and is always met with silence:
Brothers, go tell your mothers,
you know, that woman who taught you how to pray,
who taught you right from wrong,
who taught you the Ten Commandments,
who taught you the Beatitudes,
tell her that females are not to teach males.
You say you weren't a man then, just a boy—women can teach boys.
So, were her feminine lips sewn shut
the day you became a man?
Tell your mother what day that was, if you have the courage,
that she, with her God-given female brain,
stopped teaching you anything more?

Brothers, have you forgotten Deborah the prophetess
who judged and taught all Israel—men and women alike?
She was their spiritual leader. A woman.
Yes, a vessel with womanly parts.

Was she the wrong sex to lead a nation?
Did God not notice she was a woman?
Was she God's mistake?

Oh, you say that's different. That was then. This is now.

Yes, that was then, and this is now.
That is why God, being so smart, so caring,
so understanding of your male sex,
included an example in our Bible from way back, even before Deborah—
a notification from the past
to give you modern day clarification.
Remember the story of Balaam?
My Brothers, if God can voice what's what
to another stubborn man through Balaam's ass,
I say, He can use any vessel to preach truth.

Even a woman.

Arlene L. Mandell

CONSCIOUSNESS RAISING REVISITED:
WEST COAST VERSION

for Dorothy, Eva, Evelyn, Marsha, Shirley and Sue

We met every Thursday, sometimes smoked a little pot
because it was the early seventies, talked about sex, men,
money or the lack thereof. We debated whether we could be
good feminists *and* shave our legs. We pooled our kids and
resources for impromptu barbecues until each CR member
moved away, remarried or went mad.

Now in the new millennium CR rules have been revised—
We're more discreet. No one interrupts or gives advice—too
bad!

Forty years later, we earn 77 cents to a man's dollar. We
worry about kids who can't find permanent employment.
Our thighs are plumper, our faces more haggard. We talk
more about organic vegetables than orgasms.

But our Secretary of State and both California senators
Are women. Our daughters are lawyers or run their own
businesses. Our sons sometimes bathe babies *and* put down
the toilet seats for their wives or lovers.

Who says women can't change the world? Of course we can!
It's just taking a hell of a lot longer than we expected.

BIOGRAPHICAL NOTES

KIM ADDONIZIO was born in Washington, DC, and grew up in suburban Maryland, daughter of a former tennis champion mother and sports journalist father. She received her BA and MA from San Francisco State University, and has lived in the Bay Area most of her adult life, teaching private workshops and for conferences and festivals worldwide. She is the author of five poetry collections, two novels, two story collections, and two books on writing poetry—including *the Poet's Companion: A Guide to the Pleasures of Writing Poetry* (W.W. Norton, 1997), co-authored with Dorianne Laux. Her latest books are *The Palace of Illusions* (stories) and *My Black Angel: Blues Poems and Portraits*, a collaboration with woodcut artist Charles D. Jones. She volunteers with The Hunger Project, a global organization empowering the world's poorest people, especially women, to end their own hunger and poverty.

MARY ALEXANDRA AGNER is a freelance science writer working with *Paper Droids*, Argonne National Laboratory, *Under the Microscope*, and other markets; she also writes a column focusing on research results of contemporary women scientists. Her books of poetry are *The Doors of the Body* (Mayapple Press, 2009), and *The Scientific Method* (Parallel Press, 2011). Off the page, she models competence and self-confidence for the women in her corporate jobs and personal life. She holds advanced degrees in Earth & Planetary Science (M.I.T.) and Creative Writing (Emerson College), and makes her home halfway up Spring Hill.

DOROTHY ALEXANDER was raised in rural Western Oklahoma during the Depression, attended law school, and returned to practice law in small towns where she grew up. Inspired by agrarian literary traditions and populist political movements of the late 1800s and early 1900s, she chronicles the lives of rural and working class people in four poetry collections and two nonfiction works so far. She lives in Oklahoma City with her wife Devey Napier, whom she married in Santa Fe in 2013, same-sex marriage still being illegal in Oklahoma. Dorothy coordinates poetry readings for the Woody Guthrie Folk Festival in Okemah, curates the Paramount Poetry Series in OKC, reads and speaks widely, and received the 2013 Carlile Distinguished Service Award from the Oklahoma Center for the Book for service to the Oklahoma literary community.

KATHYA ALEXANDER grew up in Little Rock, daughter of a Baptist pastor who hosted Civil Rights meetings and gatherings in his church. She has worked for rape hotlines and domestic violence shelters; as Director of Employment at the Seattle Urban League, creating a job-training program for African American women transitioning from welfare to work; and as Executive Director of Justice Works!, a non-profit organization helping formerly incarcerated women reconnect with family and community and find employment. Member of the African American Writers Alliance and Seattle Storytellers Guild, Alexander is Literary Director for Seattle's Brownbox Theater, for which she has written award-winning plays staged at Seattle Rep's Poncho Theater, Seattle U's Declaration of Independents Project, and elsewhere. She has received a Hedgebrook residency, a CityArts Award, the Fringe First Award from the Edinburgh Fringe Festival, and Freehold Theater's Diversity Scholarship. She writes, teaches, and performs in Seattle.

JEFFREY ANGLES, an Associate Professor of Japanese and Translation at Western Michigan University, has translated dozens of Japan's most notable modern writers and poets. His translations have won awards from the Academy of American Poets and the Japan-U.S. Commission. He also writes his own poetry, primarily in Japanese.

TAKAKO ARAI was born in 1966 in Kiryū, Japan, where her father owned a small factory that employed mainly women to produce elaborate textiles, a traditional industry in the region. Much of Arai's poetry evokes, with surrealistic imagery and regional dialect, the lives of women factory workers she saw while growing up; her recent work focuses on how working-class women's lives have been shaped by the contemporary push toward globalization. Her poems appear in English translation in *Soul Dance: Poems by Takako Arai*, translated by Jeffrey Angles (Mi'Te Press, 2008). Arai edits the magazine *Mi'Te*, and now lives in Tokyo, where she teaches Japanese to international students at Saitama University.

WENDY BARKER taught English in Arizona high schools, then for ninth-grade in African-American West Berkeley, before returning to graduate school at UC Davis, where she was inspired by pioneering feminist scholar and poet Sandra M. Gilbert. At the University of Texas at San Antonio, as Poet-in-Residence and Professor of Creative Writing, Barker teaches numerous courses in literature by women and feminist theory. Her sixth collection, *One Blackbird at a Time: The Teaching Poems*, won the John Ciardi Prize (BkMk Press, 2015). She also has a selection of poems with accompanying essays, *Poems' Progress* (2002); a volume of co-translations (with Saranindranath Tagore) from Bengali, *Rabindranath Tagore: Final Poems* (George Braziller, 2001); and poems in many journals and anthologies, including *The Best American Poetry 2013*.

ELLEN BASS grew up in New Jersey and studied at Goucher College and at Boston University, where she studied with Anne Sexton. She co-edited, with Florence Howe, the ground-breaking *No More Masks! An Anthology of Poems by Women* (Doubleday, 1973); and co-authored, with Laura Davis, the best-selling *The Courage to Heal: A Guidebook for Women Survivors of Child Sexual Abuse* (HarperCollins, 1988, 2008). She co-founded Survivors Healing Center in Santa Cruz, California; and was founding board president of Kidpower, an international self-defense and self-empowerment organization for children and adults. Her poetry books include *Like a Beggar* (Copper Canyon Press, 2014), *The Human Line* (Copper Canyon, 2007), and *Mules of Love* (BOA Editions, 2002), which won the 2003 Lambda Literary Award for Poetry. She teaches in the MFA program in writing at Pacific University.

GRACE BAUER grew up in Pennsylvania, received an MFA in Poetry from the University of Massachusetts, worked as a librarian in New Orleans, taught at Virginia Tech in Blacksburg, then at the University of Nebraska, Lincoln since 1994, where she is Coordinator of Creative Writing and a reader for *Prairie Schooner*. At this state university, she mentors many students who, like herself, are the first in her family to attend college. Her newest book of poems is *Nowhere All At Once* (Stephen F. Austin State University Press, 2014). Previous books include *Retreats & Recognitions* (Lost Horse Press, 2007), winner of the Idaho Prize; *Beholding Eye* (CustomWords, 2006); *The Women at the Well* (Portals Press, 1997); and the anthology, *Umpteen Ways of Looking at a Possum: Critical & Creative Responses to Everette Maddox* (Xavier University Press, 2006).

SANDRA BEASLEY won the 2007 New Issues Poetry Prize for her first book, *Theories of Falling*. Her second book, *I Was the Jukebox*, appeared from W.W. Norton (2010). Poems have appeared or are forthcoming in *Black Warrior Review*, *Cave Wall*, *Blackbird*, and *Poetry*. Honors include the 2008 Poets & Writers Maureen Egan Exchange Award, the Elinor Benedict Poetry Prize, and fellowships to the Sewanee Writers' Conference, the Millay Colony, and Virginia Center for Creative Arts. Beasley serves on the Board of the Writer's Center and writes for the *Washington Post Magazine* in Washington, D.C. She is at work on a memoir, *Don't Kill the Birthday Girl: Tales from an Allergic Life*.

JAN BEATTY has four books published by the University of Pittsburgh Press: *The Switching/Yard* (2013); *Red Sugar* (2008, Paterson Poetry Prize finalist); *Boneshaker* (2002, Milton Kessler Award finalist); and *Mad River* (1995, Agnes Lynch Starrett Prize). A featured poet at the 2010 Split This Rock Poetry Festival, Beatty has been a waitress, welfare caseworker, abortion counselor, and social worker and teacher in maximum-security prisons. She is Managing Editor of MadBooks, publishing books and chapbooks by women writers. Beatty hosts and produces *Prosody*, a radio show on NPR affiliate WESA-FM featuring the work of national writers. She has lectured in writing workshops across the country, taught at the University of Pittsburgh and Carnegie Mellon University., and now directs the creative writing program at Carlow University, where she runs the Madwomen in the Attic writing workshops and teaches in the MFA program.

SHAINDEL BEERS was raised in a small town in Indiana, studied literature at Huntingdon College, Alabama (BA), and at the University of Chicago (MA) before earning her MFA in Poetry at Vermont College. She has taught at colleges and universities in Illinois and Florida but feels settled in the Eastern Oregon high-desert town of Pendleton, where she teaches at Blue Mountain Community College. She is the author of two poetry collections, *A Brief History of Time* (2009), and *The Children's War and Other Poems* (2013), both from Salt Publishing. She serves as Poetry Editor of *Contrary*. Much of her work focuses on working-class women's issues, and she enjoys mentoring young women writers since so many women writers helped her find her way.

LYTTON BELL, originally from Pennsylvania, graduated from Bryn Mawr College and later studied poetry with the legendary Molly Fisk. After several short-term jobs (fry cook, camp counselor, nursing aide, librarian), she now works as a secretary, where (to paraphrase Charles Bukowski) she makes lots of money for other people and is asked to be grateful for the opportunity to do so. She has published five books and chapbooks, including *Body Image* and *The Book of Chaps*; and has won or placed in several poetry contests, including Honorable Mention in the 2008 Wergle Flomp Humor Poetry Contest. Bell is a founding member of the Sacramento-based, all-female performance troupe, Poetica Erotica, which seeks to nurture self-esteem and to defeat stigmas of body-shame and taboo while celebrating sexual expression. Bell lives in Sacramento with her novelist husband and their two uberchildren.

Born to a Mexican mother and Jewish father, **ROSEBUD BEN-ONI** is a CantoMundo Fellow and the author of *SOLECISM* (Virtual Artists Collective, 2013). She was a Rackham Merit Fellow at the University of Michigan where she earned her MFA in Poetry, and a Horace Goldsmith Scholar at the Hebrew University of Jerusalem. Her work is forthcoming or appears in *Poetry, American Poetry Review, Arts & Letters, Bayou,* and *Puerto del Sol,* among others. She is a visiting writer for fall 2014 for the University of Texas at Brownsville's *Writers Live* Series. Rosebud is an Editorial Advisor for *VIDA: Women in Literary Arts* (vidaweb.org). She lives in Queens, New York.

JUDITH AYN BERNHARD grew up in an ethnically diverse neighborhood in the Bay Area, and worked as a Berlitz School of Languages instructor and translator. A founder and past chair of The Marin Poetry Center, and a member of the Revolutionary Poets Brigade, she is dedicated to using poetry to promote social justice and raise awareness of issues like gender equity, workers' rights, and human trafficking. Bernhard once worked as a bilingual interpreter between an Anglo building contractor and construction crews from Mexico and Central America—some of whom had quite creative work authorization documents. The job became a lesson in the politics of language and gender: she learned that some workers understood English perfectly well but preferred listening to the boss's pidgin Spanish since he signed the paychecks. Bernhard lives in San Francisco where she facilitates writing groups and participates in poetry readings.

SHEILA BLACK is the author of three poetry collections, *House of Bone, Love/Iraq* (both from CW Press) and *Wen Kroy* (Dream Horse Press), which won the Orphic Prize in Poetry. A co-editor of *Beauty is a Verb: The New Poetry of Disability* (Cinco Puntos Press), she is interested in poetics of disability and in intersections between disability and feminism. Black has worked for reproductive and health rights, educational justice and economic parity for women through The Colonias Development Council in Las Cruces, New Mexico, a non-profit that did community organizing in farmworker communities in New Mexico and West Texas. This experience has informed much of her poetry and her passion for the subject of women and work. A 2012 Witter Bynner Fellow, Black lives in San Antonio, Texas, where she directs the community literary arts center Gemini Ink.

CATHLEEN CALBERT received her B.A. from UC Berkeley, where she worked with Josephine Miles; her M.A. from Syracuse, where her thesis advisor was Philip Booth; and her Ph.D. from the University of Houston, where her dissertation advisor was Richard Howard. She has three books of poetry: *Lessons in Space*, *Bad Judgment*, and *Sleeping with a Famous Poet*; and poems in many publications, including *Feminist Studies*, *The Hudson Review*, *Ms.*, *The Paris Review*, *Poetry*, *Ploughshares*, *Rhode Island Women Speak*, *The Southern Review*, *TriQuarterly*, and *The Women's Review of Books*. She is a Professor of English at Rhode Island College.

XÁNATH CARAZA is a traveler, educator, poet and short story writer. Originally from Xalapa, Veracruz, Mexico, she has lived in Vermont and Kansas City. With an M.A. in Romance Languages, she is a lecturer in Foreign Languages and Literatures at the University of Missouri-Kansas City. Her Spanish-language books are *Conjuro* (Mammoth Publications, 2012), which received awards from the 2013 International Latino Book Awards; and *Sílabas de viento* (Mammoth, 2014). Caraza curates National Poetry Month's Poem-a-Day project for the Con Tinta Literary Organization, and has performed at Latino and Latin American poetry festivals in New York City and Los Angeles, as well as Barcelona and Granada, Spain. Inspired in her writing by women's perspectives, she is concerned about the disproportion of male and female literary voices throughout history—both as authors and characters.

SUSANA H. CASE is a Professor of Sociology and Program Coordinator at the New York Institute of Technology, where workplace issues and gender inequality are significant components of her courses. Author of several chapbooks and four full-length collections, including *Elvis Presley's Hips & Mick Jagger's Lips* (Anaphora Literary Press, 2013); *Earth and Below* (Anaphora, 2013), a collection of poems about copper mining; and most recently, *4 Rms w Vu* (Mayapple Press, 2014), Case is also a photographer, with work published widely. She received her Ph.D. from the City University of New York in 1976 and has been involved in higher education ever since. She lives in New York City with her husband.

ANN CEFOLA is author of *Face Painting in the Dark* (Dos Madres Press, 2014); *St. Agnes, Pink-Slipped* (Kattywompus Press, 2011), *Sugaring* (Dancing Girl Press, 2007), and the translation *Hence this cradle* (Seismicity Editions, 2007). She has received a Witter Bynner Poetry Translation Residency and the Robert Penn Warren Award. In 2001, she cofounded the Scarsdale Coalition on Family Violence and presented on its behalf at the first FBI conference on domestic violence. Cefola's career as a corporate writer was already launched when she pursued an MFA in Poetry at Sarah Lawrence College. Concern for classmates' school loans led her to organize panels and workshops on careers for writers and on breaking into corporate communications, which launched several women students into corporate careers. Cefola continues as a corporate writer with her company, Jumpstart, and lives in her native Scarsdale, NY, with her husband.

VICTORIA CHANG has published three books of poems: *Circle* (*Crab Orchard Review* Open Competition Award, Southern Illinois University Press, 2005); *Salvinia Molesta* (VQR Poetry Series, University of Georgia Press, 2008); and *The Boss* (McSweeney's Poetry Series, 2013). She has also edited an anthology, *Asian American Poetry: The Next Generation* (University of Illinois Press, 2004). Her poems have appeared in *Kenyon Review, American Poetry Review, Poetry, The Believer, New England Review, VQR, The Nation, New Republic, The Washington Post, Best American Poetry,* and elsewhere. She lives in Southern California with her family, and works in business.

JENNIFER CLEMENT was born in Connecticut and educated in the U.S., and has lived in Mexico much of her life. She has several books of poetry, including *The Next Stranger* (introduction by W.S. Merwin). For her new novel, the acclaimed *Prayers for the Stolen* (Hogarth, 2014) about the stealing and trafficking of young girls in rural Mexico, Clement won an NEA Fiction Fellowship and the Sara Curry Humanitarian Award; and she was named a Santa Maddalena Fellow. Other works include the novels *A True Story Based on Lies* (on the mistreatment of women servants in Mexico), a finalist for the Orange Prize; *The Poison That Fascinates*; and the memoir *Widow Basquiat*. Clement was the President of PEN Mexico from 2009-2012—her work focused on the killing of journalists in Mexico. She and her sister, Barbara Sibley, are the founding directors of The San Miguel Poetry Week.

ELAYNE CLIFT is a writer, journalist, *doula* and lecturer on women's issues. Her latest book, with Christine Morton, is *Birth Ambassadors: Doulas and the Re-emergence of Woman-Supported Birth in America*. Her novel, *Hester's Daughters* (2012), is a contemporary feminist retelling of *The Scarlet Letter*. TESOL-certified, Clift has taught in Thailand, Korea, and for universities throughout the U.S.; worked nationally and internationally as a program director, public health consultant, and educator/advocate on maternal and child health and gender issues. A Senior Correspondent for the New Delhi, India-based syndicate Women's Feature Service, and columnist and book reviewer for newspapers in New Hampshire and Vermont, she has published articles in *The Christian Science Monitor, Chronicle of Higher Education,* and *Vermont Magazine*. She lives and writes in southern Vermont.

LYN COFFIN is the award-winning author of nineteen books of poetry, fiction, drama, and translations from Russian and Georgian. She lives in Seattle and teaches Literary Fiction at the University of Washington's Department of Continuing and Professional Education. Her translation of Georgian poet Dato Barbakadze's *Still Life with Snow* received an award from the Georgian Ministry of Culture, and other volumes of translations are forthcoming. Lyn is Program Manager for Drama Queen, a group which advances the careers and well-being of women playwrights. She has done several solo performances of "Camille Claudel" at One Woman Standing (New York), 12 Minutes Max (On the Boards), Seattle Playwrights' Studio Showcase (Arts West) and elsewhere.

MARTHA COLLINS' seventh collection of poetry, *Day Unto Day*, was published by Milkweed in 2014. She has also published three volumes of co-translated Vietnamese poetry, including *Green Rice* by Lam Thi My Da (Curbstone, 2005, with Thuy Dinh).

SUSAN CORMIER, writer and filmmaker, has won or been shortlisted for CBC's National Literary Award, *Arc Magazine*'s Poem of the Year, and the Federation of B.C. Writers' Literary Writes. She has appeared in magazines including *West Coast Line*, *subTerrain*, and *Atlantis: A Women's Studies Journal*; and anthologies like *Force Field*, *Rocksalt*, and *Alive at the Center*. Her films have screened at Montreal World Film Festival, herland Feminist Film Festival, and Berlin's Zebra Poetry Film Festival. Much of Cormier's writing deals with issues of marginalization such as poverty, abuse, and mental health. A videopoem, "this bleeding place," has been used in domestic violence intervention training programs. She is currently working on a Canada Council-funded research documentary about bullying.

SHARON CUMBERLAND has had poems published in many literary journals, including *Ploughshares, Iowa Review, Image,* and *Beloit Poetry Journal.* She has been awarded *Kalliope*'s Sue Saniel Elkind Award, The Pacific Northwest Writer's Association's Zola Award for Poetry, and the Writers Haven Press Bright Side Award. *Peculiar Honors*, a full-length collection of poems, was published by Black Heron Press in 2012. Originally from Washington, DC, she spent several years as a novice in an Episcopalian Order. She lives in Seattle and directs the Creative Writing Program at Seattle University.

DARCY CUMMINGS has an M.A. in poetry from Johns Hopkins, recently completed an MFA in Creative Non-Fiction at Rutgers University Camden, and is working on a memoir and a book of poetry. Her book of poems, *The Artist As Alice: From A Photographer's Life* won the Bright Hill Press Book Award. She has taught at the University of Pennsylvania, the New Jersey Writers Project, and elsewhere—many of her students are women, including older women returning to college after many years. Cummings has received fellowships and grants from Yaddo, Virginia Center for the Creative Arts, the Dodge Foundation, and the New Jersey State Council on the Arts.

LAURA DA' is an enrolled member of the Eastern Shawnee Tribe of Oklahoma and a lifelong resident of the Pacific Northwest. Her mother broke barriers as the first journeywoman carpenter in Seattle since World War II, after many women had left war effort jobs and returned to the home front. Da' studied creative writing at the University of Washington and the Institute of American Indian Arts. Her chapbook, *The Tecumseh Motel*, appeared in *Effigies II* (Salt Press, 2014); her first book is *Tributaries* (University of Arizona Press, 2015). Da' teaches public school and lives near Seattle with her husband and son.

CORTNEY DAVIS was a nurse's aide, surgical tech, RN, and then—as one of the first nurse practitioners trained in the US—she worked for thirty-seven years, more than sixteen of these in an outpatient clinic for underserved, uninsured and undocumented women. Davis has two poetry collections, *Details of Flesh* (Calyx Books, 1997) and *Leopold's Maneuvers* (Bison Books, 2004), winner of the 2003 *Prairie Schooner* Book Prize; and two award-winning non-fiction books, *I Knew a Woman: The Experience of the Female Body* (Random House, 2001) and *The Heart's Truth: Essays on the Art of Nursing*. She is co-editor of two anthologies of poetry and prose by nurses, *Between the Heartbeats* and *Intensive Care* (both University of Iowa Press). An account of her own recent illness is *When the Nurse Becomes a Patient: A Story in Words and Images* (Kent State Univeristy Press, 2015). She lives in Connecticut.

MADELINE DEFREES has published eight poetry collections, including *Spectral Waves* (Copper Canyon, 2006) and *Blue Dusk* (Copper Canyon, 2001), which received the 2002 Lenore Marshall Poetry Prize. She spent thirty-eight years as a nun with the Sisters of the Holy Names of Jesus and Mary, entering the community at sixteen. As Sister Mary Gilbert, she earned a BA in English from Marylhurst College (1948) and an MA in Journalism from the University of Oregon (1951). She studied poetry briefly with Karl Shapiro, Robert Fitzgerald, and John Berryman; taught at Holy Names College in Spokane from 1950-1967; and resumed her baptismal name before teaching Creative Writing at the University of Montana from 1967-1979. From 1979-1985, she taught at the University of Massachusetts, Amherst. Since retiring in 1985, DeFrees has held residencies at Bucknell, Eastern Washington, and Wichita State Universities, and received NEA and Guggenheim fellowships. She lives in Portland, Oregon.

THUY DINH is a bilingual essayist and translator. With Martha Collins, she co-translated *Green Rice*, an anthology of poems by Lam Thi My Da (Curbstone, 2005), and women's poetry featured in *The Defiant Muse: Vietnamese Feminist Poems from Antiquity to the Present* (The Feminist Press at CUNY, 2008). As editor of the Vietnamese literary e-zine *Da Mau*, she and her colleagues have launched special issues on gender, pre-1975 Southern Vietnamese women's fiction, and censorship.

JENNIFER DOTSON is founder and program coordinator of Highland Park Poetry, a labor of love. Her poems have appeared in *After Hours, East on Central, Exact Change, Journal of Modern Poetry*, and the Poetic License Press anthology, *A Midnight Snack*. Her poetry collection is *Clever Gretel* (Chicago Poetry Press, 2013). A former fragrance model, she has not worn fragrance in twenty years and rarely shops in department stores. An executive assistant for a municipality, she has been informed that based on national comparisons, she is at the top of her pay scale and can expect no further growth other than small cost of living increases. She wonders, if that is so, why is it still so hard to pay the rent.

RITA DOVE, a former U.S. Poet Laureate, is the author of numerous poetry collections, most recently *Sonata Mulattica*, as well as short stories, a novel, and a play; she also edited *The Penguin Anthology of Twentieth-Century American Poetry*. In 1993, Dove was named one of ten "Outstanding Women of the Year" by *Glamour* magazine. In 1997 she received the Sara Lee Frontrunner Award; in 2003 the Emily Couric Leadership Award from the Women's Leadership Forum in Charlottesville, Virginia; and in 2012 the Women of Achievement Award from the Virginia chapter of the American Association of University Women. Other recognitions include the 1987 Pulitzer Prize in poetry, the 1996 National Humanities Medal and the 2011 National Medal of Arts. Originally from Akron, Dove is Commonwealth Professor of English at the University of Virginia.

BARBARA DRAKE began higher education in 1957 when her college had no women faculty in her field and few women graduate students. She had two small children by the time she finished graduate school, wrote high-school textbooks at home until her three children were of school age, and gained experience and eventually a full-time job in the early 1970s by offering Free University classes in feminist small press publications. In 1974 she began teaching Women's Studies at Michigan State University; and in 1983 joined the Linfield College English Department, where she developed the undergraduate creative writing program. She retired in 2007 as a Linfield Professor of English Emerita. Her newest book, a collection of personal essays, is *Morning Light* (Oregon State University Press, 2014). She lives in rural western Oregon.

PATRICIA DUBRAVA was born in New York City and raised there and in Florida until she moved to Colorado, where she earned an M.A. in English with Emphasis on Teaching Writing at the University of Colorado, Denver. She taught English and Spanish at Denver School of the Arts, concluding her career as Chair of Creative Writing. Dubrava has published two books of poems and one collection of stories translated from Spanish, and is translating a biography of an early Mexican feminist, Laura Méndez de Cuenca. She blogs at "Holding the Light," and tries to model alternatives for young women who let men determine their life decisions. She lives in Denver.

DENISE DUHAMEL'S books include *Queen for a Day: Selected and New Poems* (2001), *Two and Two* (2005), and *Ka-Ching!* (2009), all from the University of Pittsburgh Press. Her most recent, *Blowout* (University of Pittsburgh, 2013), was a finalist for the National Book Critics Circle Award and winner of a 2014 Paterson Poetry Prize. The guest editor for *The Best American Poetry 2013*, she received a 2014 Guggenheim Fellowship. One of her first jobs was in a union supermarket, with benefits and overtime pay. That supermarket no longer exists; the ones that replaced it are largely without unions. A feminist since her youth, Denise has worked in factories, restaurants, advertising firms, temp agencies, at various universities as an adjunct instructor, and is now very lucky to be a professor at Florida International University in Miami.

CAMILLE T. DUNGY is the author of *Smith Blue* (Southern Illinois University Press, 2011); *Suck on the Marrow* (Red Hen Press, 2010); and *What to Eat, What to Drink, What to Leave for Poison* (Red Hen, 2006). She edited *Black Nature: Four Centuries of African American Nature Poetry* (University of Georgia Press, 2009) and co-edited the poetry anthology *From the Fishouse* (Persea, 2009). Her honors include an American Book Award, two Northern

California Book Awards, a California Book Award silver medal, and a fellowship from the NEA. Born in Denver, raised in Southern California and Iowa, and educated at Stanford and the University of North Carolina, Greensboro. Dungy is a Professor in the English Department at Colorado State University.

SUSAN EISENBERG, poet, multi-disciplinary artist, activist and educator, explores issues of power and social policy. One of the first women in the country to become a journey-level union (IBEW) electrician, she has reframed tradeswomen's issues, calling attention in her work to the role of violence in enforcing gender and racial occupational barriers. She is author of the New York *Times* Notable Book, *We'll Call You If We Need You: Experiences of Women Working Construction*; and poetry collections *Perpetual Care, Blind Spot*, and *Pioneering*. Her touring mixed-media installation, "On Equal Terms," last exhibited at the Clemente Soto Velez Center in NYC. Her essays have appeared in *The Progressive, The Nation*, and *Utne Reader*. Graduate of Warren Wilson College's MFA program, Eisenberg taught for a decade at the University of Massachusetts Boston. She is a Resident Artist/Scholar at Brandeis University's Women's Studies Research Center.

JENNIFER FANDEL'S poetry has appeared in *Measure, RHINO, Floating Bridge Review # 7: Help Wanted, The Baltimore Review, Midwestern Gothic*; and the anthologies *Prairie Gold: An Anthology of the American Heartland*, and *A Face to Meet the Faces: An Anthology of Contemporary Persona Poetry* (University of Akron Press). Besides her day job in publishing, she believes her most important work is supporting and encouraging the work of fellow female writers. In recent years, she has directed writing workshops for women who have suffered from domestic and sexual abuse. She lives in St. Louis.

NIKKY FINNEY was born in South Carolina, daughter of a lawyer and a teacher both active in the Civil Rights Movement. Her childhood, education at Talladega College, and poetry were shaped by the activism of the Civil Rights and Black Arts Movements of the 1960s and 1970s. Finney has authored four books of poetry: *On Wings Made of Gauze* (1985), *Rice* (1995), *The World Is Round* (2003), and *Head Off & Split* (2011), which was awarded the 2011 National Book Award. After two decades as Professor of English at the University of Kentucky, she now holds a Chair in Southern Letters and Literature at the University of South Carolina. Finney also edited *The Ringing Ear: Black Poets Lean South* (2007), and co-founded the Affrilachian Poets.

KATHLEEN FLENNIKEN began her career as a civil engineer, discovering poetry in her early 30s. Her books are *Famous* (*Prairie Schooner* Poetry Prize, University of Nebraska Press, 2006), a Notable Book for the American Library Association; and *Plume* (University of Washington Press, 2012), about the Hanford Nuclear Site and her hometown of Richland, Washington, which won the Washington State Book Award. Flenniken has received a Pushcart Prize and fellowships from the NEA and Artist Trust; taught poetry through Seattle's Writers in the Schools program; and as Washington State Poet Laureate 2012-2014, visited schools and libraries throughout the state. She is an editor and president of the nonprofit Floating Bridge Press, dedicated to publishing Washington State poets; and president of Jack Straw Foundation, an audio arts studio and cultural center in Seattle.

STEFANIE FREELE was born and raised in Wisconsin. After fifteen years in corporate Human Resources, she left the world of bureaucracy to write, received an MFA in Fiction in 2008 from the Northwest Institute of Literary Arts' Whidbey Writers Workshop, and now lives with her family in Northern California. Her short story collections are *Feeding Strays* (Lost Horse Press, 2009) and *Surrounded by Water* (Press 53, 2012). She received a fellowship from *SmokeLong Quarterly*, was a Writer-In-Residence for *Necessary Fiction*, and served for several years as Fiction Editor of the *Los Angeles Review*. Stefanie's poetry and fiction can be found in *Witness*, *Glimmer Train*, *Mid-American Review*, *Western Humanities Review*, *Chattahoochee Review*, *Quarterly West*, and *American Literary Review*, among others.

SARAH FRELIGH is the author of *Sort of Gone* and *A Brief Natural History of an American Girl*, winner of the Editor's Choice Award from Accents Publishing. She has received fellowships from the NEA, Constance Saltonstall Foundation, and New York Council on the Arts. Visiting Assistant Professor of English/Creative Writing at St. John Fisher College in Rochester, New York, she held many jobs in earlier years: waitress, clerk-typist, and reporter for the Fort Myers *News-Press* and later the Philadelphia *Inquirer*. As a sportswriter assigned to cover the Miami Dolphins when most pro-sports locker rooms were closed to women, she was a plaintiff in a lawsuit that subsequently opened the Orange Bowl locker room to reporters of all genders.

DAISY FRIED has three books of poetry, all from the University of Pittsburgh Press: *She Didn't Mean to Do It* (2001), winner of the Agnes Lynch Starrett Award; *My Brother is Getting Arrested Again* (2006), finalist for the National Book Critics Circle Award; and *Women's Poetry: Poems an Advice*, named by *Library Journal* as one of the 5 Best Books of Poetry of 2013. Her poems have appeared in most major journals and *Best American Poetry 2013*. She's been awarded Guggenheim, Hodder and Pew Fellowships, a Pushcart Prize, the Cohen Award from *Ploughshares*, and *Poetry's* Editors' Prize. She reviews poetry for the *New York Times* and elsewhere, teaches in Warren Wilson College's low-residency MFA Program for Writers, and lives in South Philadelphia with her husband and daughter.

ERIN FRISTAD was born and raised along the shores and in the mountains of Washington State. She spent fifteen years as a deckhand on fishing vessels: pursuing herring near Togiak, crab off the Columbia River, salmon in more places than she can remember; and for five years in the name of science. She moved to Port Townsend, where she's worked in the boat yard and in college administration, taught creative writing, and put in many volunteer hours supporting the arts. Her poems have been published in anthologies and journals including *Rosebud*, *americas review*, *The Blue Collar Review*, *Hanging Loose*, *The Seattle Review* and *Working the Woods, Working the Sea: An Anthology of Northwest Writing*. Her chapbook, *The Glass Jar*, was released in 2013.

MARIA MAZZIOTTI GILLAN has published twenty books and co-edited four anthologies. She is the founder/executive director of the Poetry Center at Passaic County Community College in Paterson, New Jersey, where she has worked for over thirty-five years to give a voice to women writers through the Distinguished Poets Series and the *Paterson Literary Review* which she edits. At SUNY Binghamton, where she is Professor of English and directs the Binghamton Center for Writers and the creative writing program, she mentors women writers through poetry workshops. She received the 2014 George Garrett Award from AWP, the 2011 Barnes & Noble Writers for Writers Award from *Poets & Writers*, and a 2008 American Book Award for *All That Lies Between Us* (Guernica Editions).

DIANA GARCÍA was born in the San Joaquín Valley in a migrant farm labor camp, and earned a BA in English and an MFA in creative writing from San Diego State University. Her collection, *When Living Was a Labor Camp* (University of Arizona Press, 2000), won a 2001 American Book Award. García has taught for California Poets in the Schools and for San Diego-based Border Voice, and currently co-directs the Creative Writing and Social Action Program at California State University Monterey Bay. Her work—influenced by awareness of issues that affect impoverished, often minority, communities—is attuned to the sensory details and political ramifications of migrants' lives. García has read for the Poetics of Labor series at the Smithsonian's National Museum of American History; and co-edited *Fire and Ink: An Anthology of Social Action Writing* (2009).

Poet-dramatist CINDY WILLIAMS GUTIÉRREZ draws inspiration from silent and silenced voices of history and herstory. Her collection, *the small claim of bones*, is from Bilingual Press/*Editorial Bilingüe* of Arizona State University. Poems, stories, and reviews have appeared in *Calyx*; Harvard's *Journal of Feminist Studies in Religion*; *The Knotted Bond: Oregon Poets Speak of Their Sisters* (Uttered Chaos); *Letters to the World: Poems from Wom-Po Listerv* (Red Hen Press); and *VoiceCatcher: A Journal of Women's Voices & Visions*. Cindy's verse play *A Dialogue of Flower & Song* was featured in the 2012 GEMELA (Spanish and Latin American Women's Studies—pre-1800) Conference co-sponsored by the University of Portland and Portland State University. Cindy earned an MFA in Mesoamerican poetics and creative collaboration from the University of Southern Maine's Stonecoast Program. She lives in Oregon.

STEPHANIE BARBÉ HAMMER is a Professor of Comparative Literature at the University of California Riverside, where she also teaches courses on women's writing and transgender identities for Women's Studies, promoting women authors who are of color and/or of disadvantaged socio-economic groups. She is a member of the Teachers' Union and an active supporter of Anat Hoffman and Women of the Wall. Hammer received an MFA in Fiction from the Northwest Institute of Literary Arts in 2012, and has published the poetry chapbook *Sex with Buildings* (Dancing Girl Press, 2012) and the full-length collection *How Formal?* (Spout Hill Press, 2014). She and her husband divide their time between Los Angeles and Coupeville, Washington, on Whidbey Island.

JANICE N. HARRINGTON grew up in Alabama and Nebraska—both those settings, especially rural Alabama, figure in her writing. She has worked as a public librarian and a professional storyteller nationwide, including at the National Storytelling Festival. Her poetry books are *Even the Hollow My Body Made Is Gone* (BOA, 2007), which won the A. Poulin, Jr., Poetry Prize and the Kate Tufts Discovery Award; and *The Hands of Strangers: Poems from the Nursing Home* (BOA, 2011). Harrington has received a NEA Fellowship for Poetry and a Rona Jaffe Foundation Writers' Award for emerging women writers. Her children's books have won many awards and citations, and her poetry appears regularly in American literary magazines. She now teaches creative writing at the University of Illinois.

JANA HARRIS was born in San Francisco, raised in the Pacific Northwest, and worked for six years as director of Writers in Performance at the Manhattan Theatre Club. She now lives with her husband in the foothills of the Cascades, raising horses and practicing equestrian dressage. Her poetry collections include *Manhattan as a Second Language*; and *The Dust of Everyday Life: An Epic Poem of the Pacific Northwest*, on the lives of forgotten Northwest pioneers, particularly women. Her memoir is *Horses Never Lie About Love* (Simon & Schuster, 2011). Her new book is *You Haven't Asked About My Wedding or What I Wore; Poems of Courtship on the American Frontier* (University of Alaska Press, 2014). Founder and editor of *Switched-on Gutenberg*, a longstanding online poetry journal, she teaches poetry online for the University of Washington.

SHARON HASHIMOTO has been a writing instructor at Highline College for over twenty years. Her poetry collection, *The Crane Wife* (Story Line Press, 2003), was co-winner of the Nicholas Roerich Prize; stories and poems have appeared in *The American Scholar*, *Crab Orchard Review*, *North American Review*, *Poetry*, *Raven Chronicles*, *Shenandoah* and others. In 1990, she received a Poetry Fellowship from the NEA. For many years, she has been grateful to support young women writers through the Cottages at Hedgebrook. A Seattle-area native, she lives with her family in Tukwila, south of Seattle.

LINDA M. HASSELSTROM became a feminist when she read the first issue of *Ms. Magazine*. She began working on her family's South Dakota cattle ranch when she was ten, and she has continued ranching while directing Windbreak House Writing retreats, established in 1996 for women (now open to men). Hasselstrom's writing has appeared in many books, anthologies, and magazines. *Dirt Songs: A Plains Duet* (with Twyla M. Hansen) won the Nebraska Book Award for Poetry in 2012 and was a finalist for the High Plains Book awards and Women Writing the West's WILLA award. *Bitter Creek Junction* won the Wrangler for Best Poetry from Oklahoma City's National Cowboy & Western Heritage Museum.

LINDA HOGAN (Chickasaw) is a former Writer in Residence for The Chickasaw Nation, Professor Emerita of Creative Writing (the second minority woman to become a full professor) from the University of Colorado, and an internationally recognized author, environmentalist, and public speaker. She has published award-winning novels and essay collections, edited anthologies on the environment and Native spiritual traditions, written scripts for PBS documentaries, and received fellowships from the NEA, Guggenheim and Lannan Foundations. *Dark. Sweet.: New & Selected Poems* (Coffee House Press, 2014), includes work from seven earlier collections. Born in Denver and educated in Colorado, Hogan held professorships in American Indian Studies at the universities of Minnesota and Oklahoma before returning to teach in Colorado. She has worked with at-risk Native teens and youth in horse programs, and she now lives and writes in the Colorado mountains.

CATHY PARK HONG grew up in Los Angeles, and studied at Oberlin College (BA) and the Iowa Writers' Workshop (MFA). Her books of poetry are *Translating Mo'um* (Hanging Loose Press, 2002); *Dance Dance Revolution* (Barnard Women Poets Prize, W.W. Norton, 2007); and *Engine Empire* (Norton, 2012). Hong has received Fulbright, NEA, and New York Foundation for the Arts Fellowships, and her poems have appeared in *A Public Space, Poetry, Paris Review, Conjunctions, McSweeney's, APR, Harvard Review, Boston Review,* and *The Nation.* She is an Associate Professor at Sarah Lawrence College and regular faculty at the Queens MFA Program in Charlotte, North Carolina.

CAROLINA HOSPITAL is a poet, novelist, and professor at Miami Dade College where she has received two Endowed Teaching Chairs. She left Cuba as a child with her parents who sought refuge in the US. Her collection, *The Child of Exile: A Poetry Memoir* (Arte Público Press, 2004), explores this experience. Hospital has published seven books, including a freshman composition guide; and a novel, *A Little Love* (under the name C.C. Medina), about four professional Latinas. Through her teaching and publications, including the translation of *Everyone Will Have to Listen* by Cuban poet and political prisoner Tania Díaz Castro, she has worked to broaden perceptions and prospects of women, particularly Latino women, in the workplace and society as a whole. She lives in Miami.

HOLLY J. HUGHES is author of *Sailing by Ravens* (University of Alaska Press, 2014); co-author of *The Pen and the Bell: Mindful Writing in a Busy World* (Skinner House Press, 2012); and editor of the award-winning anthology, *Beyond Forgetting: Poetry and Prose about Alzheimer's Disease* (Kent State University Press, 2009). She has taught writing at Edmonds Community College for more than twenty-five years, and at regional conferences and workshops, including the FisherPoets Gathering in Astoria. Having spent over thirty summers on the water in Alaska—commercial fishing for salmon, skippering a sixty-five-foot schooner, and working as a ship's naturalist—she enjoys connecting and sharing her writing with the many women who now work in commercial fishing.

LUISA A. IGLORIA grew up in the Philippines, where her mother was an early advocate and activist for family planning—a radical, progressive stance in the 1960s. Luisa was educated at the University of the Philippines, Ateneo de Manila University, and the University of Illinois Chicago as a 1992-1995 Fulbright Fellow. Her thirteen books include *Ode to the Heart Smaller than a Pencil Eraser* (2014 May Swenson Prize); *Night Willow: Prose Poems* (Phoenicia Publishing, 2014); *Juan Luna's Revolver* (2009 Ernest Sandeen Prize); and *Trill & Mordent* (WordTech Editions, 2005). As a writer of color and mother of four daughters, she has striven to teach her children and students to develop their capabilities, despite a world which might seek to marginalize them. She directs the Creative Writing Program at Old Dominion University, and lives in Norfolk with her family.

ARLITIA JONES is a poet and playwright in Anchorage, where she spends nights and weekends writing, and weekdays working full-time in her family's wholesale butcher shop. She's co-founder of TossPot Productions, a theatre company committed to providing equitable roles for women on stage; and author of *The Bandsaw Riots* (Bear Star Press, 2001), winner of the Dorothy Brunsman Poetry Prize. In 2014 her play, *Rush at Everlasting*, about two women plotting to rob a bank in the 1930s, premiered at Perseverance Theatre; and *Come to Me, Leopards*, about a women's cross-country running team, received a workshop production at Cyrano's Theatre in Anchorage. She is a member of the Seattle Repertory Theatre's Writers Group and a recent alumna of Hedgebrook, where she completed a draft of her latest play about Mother Jones.

VANDANA KHANNA was born in New Delhi, India and attended the University of Virginia and Indiana University, where she earned her MFA. She taught in the UCLA Extension Writers' Program while her children were small, and she is now a lecturer in English at the University of Southern California. Her collections are *Train to Agra* (*Crab Orchard Review* First Book Prize, SIU Press), and *Afternoon Masala* (Miller Williams Poetry Prize co-winner, University of Arkansas Press, 2014). Khanna's work has appeared in journals such as *Crazyhorse, Callaloo* and *The Indiana Review*, and the anthologies *Asian American Poetry: The Next Generation* and *Indivisible: An Anthology of Contemporary South Asian American Poetry*. Her work often explores the dynamics of gender and domesticity within the framework of immigration and expatriation.

CAROLYN ASHLEY KIZER—born 1924 in Spokane, Washington—is a major American poet of the Pacific Northwest whose works reflect her feminism. She is the author of eight books of poetry, including *Cool, Calm & Collected* (Copper Canyon Press, 2000); *Harping On* (1996); *Yin* (1984), which won the 1985 Pulitzer Prize; *Mermaids in the Basement: Poems for Women* (1984); *Midnight Was My Cry* (1971); *Knock Upon Silence* (1965); and *The Ungrateful Garden* (1961). In 1959, at the University of Washington in Seattle, she co-founded *Poetry Northwest* and served as its editor until 1965. Kizer was the only woman in the seminal anthology, *Five Poets of the Pacific Northwest* (University of Washington Press, 1964). She was a Specialist in Literature for the US State Department in Pakistan from 1965-1966; and from 1966-1970, the first Director of the Literature Program of the NEA. Recipient of an American Academy of Arts and Letters award, the Frost Medal, and the Theodore Roethke Poetry Award; and a former Chancellor of the Academy of American Poets, she lived in Sonoma, California, and Paris, until her passing on October 9, 2014.

MELISSA KWASNY is the author of five poetry books: *Pictograph* (2015); The *Nine Senses* (Milkweed Editions, 2011), *Reading Novalis in Montana* (Milkweed, 2009); *Thistle* (The Idaho Prize for Poetry, Lost Horse Press, 2006), and *The Archival Birds* (Bear Star, 2000). Her collection of nonfiction is *Earth Recitals: Essays on Image and Vision* (Lynx House Press, 2013). She edited *Toward the Open Field: Poets on the Art of Poetry 1800-1950* (Wesleyan University Press, 2004); and co-edited *I Go to the Ruined Place: Contemporary Poets in Defense of Global Human Rights* (Lost Horse, 2009). Originally from Indiana, Kwasny lives in western Montana. After a series of blue-collar jobs in earlier years, she teaches for Carroll College in Helena, and as a visiting poet for universities, conferences, and residencies nationwide.

LAM THI MY DA was born in 1949, near the scene of heavy fighting during the Vietnam-American War. She has published six collections of poems in Viet Nam, won several major prizes for poetry; and also published three collections of stories for children. *Green Rice*, a bilingual collection of her poems with co-translations by Martha Collins and Thuy Dinh, was published by Curbstone in 2005. She lives in Hue, in central Viet Nam.

BARBARA LAMORTICELLA moved from San Francisco to Oregon with her husband in the late 1960s, lives on rural acreage near Portland, and is active in the Oregon women's writing community. As host of "Talking Earth," a poetry program on KBOO-FM, she has featured many women poets; organized readings for International Women's Day and other occasions; and directed several writing groups for women. After a residency at the Soapstone Writing Retreat for Women, she helped to evaluate subsequent Soapstone applications. She was honored with the first award specifically for Women Writers given by the Oregon Literary Association.

DORIANNE LAUX grew up in Maine and worked as a cook, gas station manager, maid, and donut holer before receiving a BA in English from Mills College in 1988. Her books include *Awake, What We Carry* (finalist for the National Book Critic's Circle Award), and *Smoke*—all from BOA Editions. Other books are *Facts about the Moon* (W. W. Norton, 2005; Oregon Book Award); *The Book of Men* (Norton, 2011); and *The Book of Women* (Red Dragonfly Press, 2012). Co-author with Kim Addonizio of *The Poet's Companion: A Guide to the Pleasures of Writing Poetry*, Laux has received Pushcart Prizes and fellowships from the NEA and Guggenheim Foundation. She and her husband, poet Joseph Millar, taught for several years in the University of Oregon's MFA program, and since 2008 in the MFA program at North Carolina State University in Raleigh. She works through teaching, "to ensure every girl or woman in my class has a voice, . . . to articulate, through poetry, their life on earth."

KATE LEBO is a feminist who writes at the intersection of literature and food. She's the author of two books on the art of pie-making, *Pie School* and *A Commonplace Book of Pie*. Her zine *The Pie Lady's Manifesto* (eight pieces on food writing, feminism, sexual harassment, and Sylvia Plath) was republished by *The Rumpus* in 2014. Her poems and essays have appeared in *Best New Poets, New England Review, Gastronomica, Willow Springs,* and *Poetry Northwest,* among other journals. She founded Pie School, her roaming pastry academy, after receiving her MFA from the University of Washington, and she teaches creative writing workshops nationally.

DONNA J. GELAGOTIS LEE earned a B.A. *cum laude* in English/Creative Writing from Sweet Briar College, where she was a Davison-Foreman scholar. She lived in Athens, Greece, for many years, and has worked as a freelance editor. Her book, *On the Altar of Greece* (Gival Press Poetry Award; 2007 Eric Hoffer Book Award: Notable for Art) was nominated for a *Los Angeles Times* Book Award. Her poetry has appeared in *The Bitter Oleander, CALYX, Cimarron Review, Feminist Studies, Jacket, The Massachusetts Review,* and *Women's Studies Quarterly.* She has often focused on women's roles and women's work, especially in her writing set in Greece.

MIA LEONIN has two books of poetry, *Braid* and *Unraveling the Bed* (Anhinga Press), and a memoir, *Havana and Other Missing Fathers* (University of Arizona Press). She has received an Academy of American Poets Prize, Florida Individual Artist Fellowships, and Money for Women grants from the Barbara Deming Memorial Fund. Her work has appeared in *Alaska Quarterly Review, Chelsea, Indiana Review, Prairie Schooner, River Styx,* and *Witness,* and has been nominated for the Pushcart Prize. She teaches creative writing at the University of Miami, and as literary artist in residence has conducted bilingual (English - Spanish) poetry workshops for mothers and daughters at Miami's Deering Estate.

SARAH LINDSAY was born in Cedar Rapids, Iowa; graduated from St. Olaf College (BA in English and Creative Writing), and received an MFA from the University of North Carolina-Greensboro. She has two books in the Grove Press Poetry Series: *Primate Behavior,* a finalist for the National Book Award, and *Mount Clutter;* and two volumes from Copper Canyon Press, *Twigs & Knucklebones* (2008), and *Debt to the Bone-Eating Snotflower* (2014). She has received a Lannan Literary Fellowship and a Pushcart Prize, and works as a copy editor in Greensboro.

LAURA RUTH LOOMIS has been a social worker doing child protective work in the San Francisco area for more than twenty years. Her poetry has appeared in *Family Matters, The Pagan's Muse,* and *Workers Write: Tales from the Couch.*

DEBORAH MAJORS is an Associate Pastor of a congregation whose Senior Pastor is also a woman. Her work has been published in *Blackwater Review, Barefoot Review, The Dead Mule School of Southern Literature, Deep South Magazine, ellipsis . . . literature and art, Big River Poetry Review,* and *A Touch of Saccharine Anthology* (A Kind of Hurricane Press). When she's not working or writing, she enjoys open mic nights, hosting family gatherings, and helping women be all that they can be, spiritually and otherwise. A wife and mother of two grown sons, she lives on thirty rural acres in the Florida Panhandle.

MARY MAKOFSKE is the author of *Traction* (Richard Snyder Prize, Ashland Poetry Press, 2011), *The Disappearance of Gargoyles*, and the chapbook *Eating Nasturtiums* (Flume Press). "Higher Education, 1970" describes the first time she realized that degrees and professionalism would not guarantee a woman equal treatment. Makofske has been a long-time supporter of women's rights organizations including NOW, the Ms. Foundation for Women, and NARAL; and she worked for several years as a health educator for Planned Parenthood. She lives north of New York City.

ARLENE MANDELL is a retired professor from William Paterson University in New Jersey, where she taught literature, poetry and women's studies. Her poems, essays, and short stories appear widely in newspapers and literary magazines. Now living in Santa Rosa, California, she is an active member of the American Association of University Women, for whom she has planned numerous literary and fundraising events. At her first job, as a secretary at NYU when she was sixteen, she earned $54 a week, but was permitted to take eight free credits per semester. At thirty-one she was a staff writer at *Good Housekeeping*, earning $10,000 a year. She applauds all efforts to pay women what they are worth.

ELLEN MAYOCK, a Professor of Spanish and Women's and Gender Studies at Washington and Lee University, has published a book on 20th century Spanish women writers; a translation of a one-act play (by Chris Gavaler), "Man Woman *Hombre Mujer*"; and over thirty articles on Spanish, Latin American, and US-Latina literature. She is also co-editor of several scholarly works. Mayock's poems in Spanish appear in *Letras Femeninas* and in the anthology, *Fronteras de lo imposible (Casa de los Poetas,* 2014). She oversees Washington and Lee's volunteer organization, English for Speakers of Other Languages (ESOL), where she works with Spanish-speaking women and their children on issues like immigration policy, domestic violence, literacy and education.

OCTAVIA MCBRIDE-AHEBEE is from Philadelphia, where she works as a teacher. She lived several years in Cote d'Ivoire and taught at the International Community School of Abidjan. Her work has appeared in *Damazine; Yellow Medicine; Fingernails Across the Chalkboard: Poetry and Prose on HIV/AIDS From the Black Diaspora; Under Our Skin: Literature of Breast Cancer; Sea Breeze: A Journal of Contemporary Liberian Writing, JAMA; International Quarterly*; and *Beloit Poetry Journal*. Poetry collections are *Assuming Voices* (Lit Pot Press, 2003) and *Where My Birthmark Dances* (Finishing Line, 2011). Her poetry gives voice to women who historically have not been heard: African women, women in refugee camps, victims of civil war, women who battle health challenges like obstetric fistula and breast cancer, immigrant women trying to find a place in their adopted countries. It increasingly addresses the environmental devastation created by corporate development.

KATHLEEN McCLUNG, author of *Almost the Rowboat*, has work in *Mezzo Cammin, Ekphrasis, Atlanta Review, The Healing Muse, PMS: poemmemoirstory, A Bird Black as the Sun: California Poets on Crows and Ravens*, and elsewhere. Winner of the Rita Dove Poetry Prize,

McClung has been a finalist for several awards, serves as the sonnet sponsor/judge for the Soul-Making Keats competition, and is a member of the Bay Area Women's Poetry Salon. She has worked as a book editor, and teaches at the Writing Salon and Skyline College, where she mentors students in the Women in Transition learning community and directs *Women on Writing: WOW Voices Now*, celebrating California writers of all ages. She lives in San Francisco.

COLLEEN J. MCELROY, Professor Emeritus at the University of Washington, has nine collections of poems, including *Here I Throw Down My Heart* (2012), a finalist for Binghamton University's Milton Kessler Award, and the Phillis Wheatley/Harlem Book Award. Besides a 1985 American Book Award and the 2008 PEN Oakland Literary Award, she has received fellowships from the NEA and the Fulbright Foundation. Her poems appear in *Best American Poetry*, *The Oxford Anthology of African American Poetry*, poetryfoundation.org, and numerous literary magazines. Poems of hers have been translated into Arabic, French, German, Greek, Italian, Malay, and Serbo-Croatian. She lives in Seattle.

KRISTEN MCHENRY is a poet and fiction writer who lives and works in Seattle. Her work appears in publications including *Busk, Tiferet, Big Pulp, Dark Matter*, and the anthology, *Many Trails to the Summit*. Her chapbooks are *The Goatfish Alphabet* (Naissance Press, 2010), and *Triplicity: Poems in Threes* (Indigo Ink Press, 2011). A pair of short stories was published as *Tender Vessels* (Loyal Stone Press, 2013); and *The Acme Employee Handbook* appeared from Jaffa Press in 2014. Kristen donates to Women for Women International, an organization that provides women survivors of war and other conflicts with the resources to move from crisis and poverty to stability and self-sufficiency.

COLLEEN MICHAELS directs the Writing Studio at Montserrat College of Art in Beverly, Massachusetts, where she hosts The Improbable Places Poetry Tour. Her poems have appeared in *Barrelhouse, poetrymagazine.com, Cider Press Review, Paper Nautilus*; in the anthologies *Here Come the Brides: Reflections on Love and Lesbian Marriage* (Seal Press, 2012), and *Modern Grimmoire: Fairy Tales, Fables and Folklore* (Indigo Ink Press, 2013); received Honorable Mention in the Allen Ginsberg Poetry competition; and been made into installations for the Massachusetts Poetry Festival, and the Peabody Essex Museum. At SUNY Fredonia, her graduate thesis, *Devil in a Green Dress*—focusing on women's roles in Celtic and Medieval Arthurian Literature—was recognized for its excellence in research on women.

HELENA MINTON has been a public librarian for thirty years, first in reference, then as an Assistant Director, and the past twelve as a Director—engaging with her community and working with many dedicated and innovative women to ensure that libraries thrive. Before that, she was an adjunct English instructor, substitute teacher, and office temp; she completed an MFA in Poetry at the University of Massachusetts. Her poetry collections include *The Canal Bed* (Alice James Books, 1985); and *The Gardener and* *the Bees* (March Street Press, 2006). Poems have appeared in journals and anthologies, including *The Beloit Poetry Journal, Parting Gifts, ROAR*, and *Sojourner: A Feminist Anthology*. Minton lives and work near Boston.

BONNIE J. MORRIS is a women's studies professor at both George Washington and Georgetown Universities in Washington, D.C. In college, she went door-to-door for the Equal Rights Amendment, and earned her Ph.D. in Women's History from Binghamton University. She has published eleven books on women's history and cultural identity, including three Lambda Literary Award finalists (for *Girl Reel, Eden Built by Eves*, and *Revenge of the Women's Studies Professor*). Her *Women's History for Beginners* was featured in 2014 on C-Span Book TV and won second prize in the New England Book Festival. "Dr. Bon" (as students call her) has served as scholarly advisor to the National Women's History Museum, as a board member/emcee for Mothertongue (D.C.'s spoken-word stage for women), and as a worker at women's music festivals nationwide.

THYLIAS MOSS grew up in Cleveland in a working-class family of African American, Native, and European heritage; and was educated at Syracuse, Oberlin and the University of New Hampshire. She has been active in Planned Parenthood since being raped in her teens. After some years of office work, she taught at Phillips Academy in Massachusetts, and she is now Professor of English and Art and Design at the University of Michigan. She has published ten books, two nominated for the National Book Critics Circle Award. Known for wide-ranging, increasingly experimental work, and for dramatic readings, Moss has received NEA, Guggenheim, and MacArthur Fellowships. Her most recent book, *Tokyo Butter* (Persea Books, 2006), is a collection of "poams" ("products of acts of making," integrating poetry, film, sound, and computer science).

LESLÉA NEWMAN is the author of sixty books. She has received poetry fellowships from the Massachusetts Artists Foundation and the NEA, and the James Baldwin Award for Cultural Achievement. Nine of her books have been Lambda Literary Award finalists. She wrote *Heather Has Two Mommies*, the first children's book to portray lesbian families in a positive way, and has followed up this pioneering work with several more children's books on lesbian and gay families, and books for adults about lesbian identity, Jewish identity, AIDS, eating disorders, butch/femme relationships, and sexual abuse. Her award-winning short story, "A Letter to Harvey Milk," has been made into a film and adapted for the stage. Newman is a popular guest lecturer, speaking on college campuses nationwide. She has taught fiction writing at Clark University, and is a faculty mentor at Spalding University's brief-residency MFA Program in Writing.

CAROLE SIMMONS OLES is the author of nine books of poems, two of them based on the lives of distinguished American women, as well as poems in most major literary magazines. Her most recent book is *A Selected History of Her Heart*. For many summers, she taught at Bread Loaf Writers' Conference and the School of English at Middlebury College. Since 1992, Oles has taught at California State University Chico, where she is Professor Emerita. Her first workspace was the kitchen table in her parents' three-room apartment in Queens; she now writes in Chico at a schoolteacher's desk from her children's closed elementary school. Her fourteenth summer she typed mailing labels for the Business and Professional Women's Association in a stuffy, cramped room in midtown Manhattan.

JACQUELINE OSHEROW is the author of seven books of poetry, most recently *Ultimatum from Paradise* (LSU Press, 2014). She has received fellowships from the Guggenheim Foundation, the NEA, the Ingram Merrill Foundation, the Witter Bynner Prize from the American Academy and Institute of Arts and Letters, and several prizes from the Poetry Society of America. With three daughters, she strives to be a feminist by example. Raised in Philadelphia and educated at Radcliffe and Princeton, she is Distinguished Professor of English at the University of Utah.

MIRANDA PEARSON is the author of four collections of poetry from Oolichan Books: *Prime* (2001); *The Aviary* (2007); *Harbour* (2009), which was shortlisted for the BC Book Prize for Poetry; and *The Fire Extinguisher* (2015). She holds an MFA from the University of British Columbia, and has taught poetry both there and at Simon Fraser University. She has been a Psychiatric Nurse for 25 years, with particular focus on women's mental health, and facilitates poetry workshops in health care settings.

LUCIA PERILLO grew up near New York City, graduated from McGill University with a major in wildlife management, and worked for the U.S. Fish and Wildlife Service. She completed her MA in English at Syracuse while working seasonally at Mount Rainer National Park; moved to Olympia, Washington, in 1987; and taught at Saint Martin's College. In the 1990s, Perillo taught creative writing at Southern Illinois University. Her six books of poetry include *On the Spectrum of Possible Deaths* (Copper Canyon Press, 2012), finalist for the National Book Critics' Circle Award; and *Inseminating the Elephant* (Copper Canyon, 2009), finalist for the Pulitzer Prize and winner of the Library of Congress's Bobbitt Prize. Her essay collection is *I've Heard the Vultures Singing: Field Notes on Poetry, Illness, and Nature* (2007); her book of short stories, *Happiness Is a Chemical in the Brain.* She lives in Olympia with her husband.

RHONDA PETTIT is a poet, scholar, and professor of English and Women's Studies at the University of Cincinnati—Blue Ash. Her poetic drama examining sex slavery and consumerism, *The Global Lovers*, was a Critic's Pick at the 2010 Cincinnati Fringe Festival. She has a chapbook, *Fetal Waters* (2012), and poems in literary magazines. Her scholarship concerning Dorothy Parker produced two books, *A Gendered Collision* (2000) and *The Critical Waltz* (2005), and she served as poetry editor for the first two volumes of *The Aunt Lute Anthology of U.S. Women Writers* (2004, 2006). She teaches writing and literature courses focused on human rights and social justice, among these Women's Prison Writing.

JO PITKIN earned a BA from Kirkland College and an MFA from the Iowa Writers' Workshop. She is the author of *The Measure* (Finishing Line Press), *Cradle of the American Circus: Poems from Somers, New York* (The History Press), and *Commonplace Invasions* (Salmon Poetry); and editor of *Lost Orchard: Prose and Poetry from the Kirkland College Community* (SUNY Press). Buoyed by the second wave of feminism, Jo marched for the ERA, served as the first female editor of Kirkland College's literary magazine, and was the first paid staff member at Alice James Books. Since 1983, she has run a freelance business, writing K-12 educational materials, including biographical sketches for America's Notable Women Series (Apprentice Shop Books). Jo lives and works in the Hudson River Valley.

MEREDITH QUARTERMAIN, poet and story writer, lives in Vancouver, BC. *Vancouver Walking* won a BC Book Award; *Recipes from the Red Planet* was a finalist for this award; and *Nightmarker* was a finalist for a Vancouver Book Award. *Rupert's Land: A Novel* explores aboriginal/settler relations in dustbowl Alberta; a new collection of stories is *I, Bartleby* (2015). In 2002, she cofounded Nomados Literary Publishers, printing innovative Canadian and US chapbooks. As a publisher she seeks writing by women to increase women's participation in public conversation. Her reward is seeing these publications win a prize or a job promotion for their authors. Quartermain convenes a monthly gathering for women writers to network, problem-solve, share work, and help overcome male-centred bias.

LOIS RED ELK is an enrolled member of the Fort Peck Sioux in Montana, descended on her father's side from the Sitting Bull family. Raised in her traditional culture, she is a quill and bead worker, traditional dancer, and advocate for cultural preservation and practice. During her years in Los Angeles, she was a talk show host, technical advisor for television and films, and actor with roles in *Skins*, *Lakota Woman*, *Ishii: the Last of His Tribe*, and over two dozen other films and series. She has worked on many Native American anthologies and magazines, wrote a weekly column for her tribe's newspaper, and teaches traditional cultural arts courses she developed at Fort Peck Community College. Her first book, *Our Blood Remembers* (Many Voices Press, 2011), won the Best Nonfiction award from Wordcraft Circle of Native Writers and Storytellers; her poetry collection is *Dragonfly Weather* (Lost Horse Press, Native American Poets' Series, 2013).

HELEN RICKERBY is from Wellington, New Zealand, where she works as a web editor. Her second collection, *My Iron Spine* (2008), features biographical poems about women from history, many of whom have been largely forgotten. She is co-managing editor of *JAAM*, one of the few literary magazines in New Zealand to be edited by women; and she directs Seraph Press, a boutique publisher that focuses on women poets. Her most recent collection is *Cinema* (Mākaro Press, 2014).

JUDITH ROCHE is the author of four poetry collections, most recently *Wisdom of the Body* (Black Heron Press, 2007), an American Book Award winner; and *All Fire All Water* (Black Heron, 2015). She has published widely in literary magazines, has poems installed as part of several Seattle-area public art projects, has taught at various universities, and conducts poetry workshops throughout the country. From a strongly union activist family in Detroit, Roche worked on the Alaska pipeline, and after moving to Seattle, served as the literary director of One Reel, the company that produces Bumbershoot, Seattle's Labor Day weekend arts and cultural festival. She lives in Seattle.

KATE RUSHIN is the author of *The Black Back-Ups* and "The Bridge Poem." With a BA from Oberlin College and an MFA in Creative Writing from Brown University, she has taught poetry writing at MIT, UMASS-Boston and Wesleyan, where she directed The Center for African American Studies. She has held fellowships from the Fine Arts Work Center in Provincetown and Cave Canem. Her work appears in *Callaloo*; *Sister/Citizen: Shame, Stereotypes and Black Women in America* (Yale University Press); *Sunken Garden Poetry* (Wesleyan University Press); and in features on NPR. Kate worked for ten years as a member of the New Words Bookstore Collective in Cambridge, Massachusetts, and as a member of Boston Women's Community Radio, producing and hosting "The Women's Talk Show" on WRBB. She lives in Connecticut.

RIKKI SANTER has worked as a journalist, a magazine and book editor, a poet-in-the-schools, co-founder and managing editor of an alternative newspaper, and her all-time favorite: bagel street vendor. She was inspired by her mother, a theatre producer who directed her all-male staff with finesse in an era when women answered to men. Santer earned a MA in journalism from Kent State University and a MFA from Ohio State University. She lives in Columbus, Ohio, where she teaches literature, writing, and film studies at Upper Arlington High School. Her chapbook is *Clothesline Logic* (Pudding House Press, 2009); her latest collection is *Fishing for Rabbits* (Kattywompus Press, 2013); she has won the Best of Ohio Writer Contest.

PENELOPE SCAMBLY SCHOTT is the author of a novel, nine poetry books, and six chapbooks. Her verse biography *A is for Anne: Mistress Hutchinson Disturbs the Commonwealth* won the Oregon Book Award, *Baiting the Void* won the Orphic Award, and *Crow Mercies* received the Sarah Lantz Memorial Prize. Most recent is *Lillie Was a Goddess, Lillie Was a Whore*, a study of prostitution, past and present. Originally from New Jersey—where early jobs included selling cosmetics, making donuts, and caring for the elderly as a home health aide—Penelope earned a Ph.D. in Late Medieval English Literature and taught literature and creative writing at Rutgers University and other colleges. Penelope now lives with her husband in Portland, and in the tiny eastern Oregon town of Dufur, where she teaches an annual poetry workshop.

WILLA SCHNEBERG is a poet, visual artist, and social worker in private practice in Portland, Oregon. She has authored five poetry collections, including *In the Margins of the World*, recipient of the Oregon Book Award; and *Rending the Garment*, a series of linked poems about a Jewish-American family. Schneberg feels she makes a difference when women clients become strong enough to leave abusive situations and report their harassers; come to believe in their professional abilities and break the glass ceiling at their workplaces; or realize that their challenges are unique but also result from a sexist/classist/racist/ageist culture. Clients with such awareness can gain confidence and heal.

ELAINE SEXTON has held executive positions in magazine publishing throughout her professional life, most recently as Senior Editor at *ARTnews*. Her collections of poetry are *Sleuth* (2003) and *Causeway* (2008), both from New Issues Press; and *Prospect/Refuge* (Sheep Meadow Press, 2015). Poems and reviews have appeared in *Art in America, American Poetry Review, Oprah Magazine, Poetry*, and *The Women's Review of Books*. She received an MFA from Sarah Lawrence College, and teaches poetry workshops there and at New York University. About work with women, she says: "As a poet, critic, and teacher I support women artist and writer colleagues, teaching their poetry and art, reviewing their work, and interviewing them in print and online. In over twenty years in magazine publishing, I have actively hired and mentored women in the workplace."

LAURA SHOVAN is poetry editor of *Little Patuxent Review* and of *Life in Me Like Grass on Fire: Love Poems* (MWA Books, 2011); and co-editor of *Voices Fly: An Anthology of Exercises and Poems from the Maryland State Arts Council Artists-in-Residence Program*, for which she teaches. Laura has been a Rita Dove Poetry Award finalist, and received a scholarship to the *Gettysburg Review* Conference for Writers. Her chapbook, *Mountain, Log, Salt and Stone*, won the Harriss Poetry Prize (CityLit Press, 2010); her debut novel-in-verse for children—in which fifth graders organize to fight the demolition of their school—is forthcoming from Wendy Lamb Books (Random House, 2016).

SANDY SHREVE edited *Working for a Living*, an anthology of writing by women about work (Room of One's Own, 1988); and co-edited *In Fine Form—The Canadian Book of Form Poetry* (Polestar Press, 2005). Her poetry books include *Waiting for the Albatross* (Oolichan Books, 2014), *Suddenly, So Much* (Exile Editions, 2005), and *Belonging* (Sono Nis Press, 1997). Now retired, Sandy was a long-time activist with the Association of University and College Employees, an independent feminist union representing clerical and technical staff at Simon Fraser University; and a student advisor and administrator for the SFU Women Studies Department's credit and community outreach programs. She founded British Columbia's Poetry in Transit program and helped organize the first Mayworks festivals in Vancouver, BC.

MARTHA SILANO has four books of poetry: *What the Truth Tastes Like, Blue Positive, The Little Office of the Immaculate Conception* (winner of the 2010 Saturnalia Books Poetry Prize), and *Reckless Lovely* (Saturnalia, 2014). She co-edited *The Daily Poet: Day-By-Day Prompts for Your Writing Practice* (Two Sylvias Press, 2013). Her poems have appeared in *Poetry, Orion, Paris Review, APR*, and *North American Review*, where she received the 2014 James Hearst Poetry Prize; and in anthologies including *American Poetry: The Next Generation* and *The Best American Poetry 2009*. Martha has received fellowships from the University of Arizona Poetry Center, Washington State Artist Trust, 4Culture, and the Seattle Office of Arts

& Culture. She edits *Crab Creek Review*; curates Beacon Bards, a Seattle-based reading series; and teaches at Bellevue College, striving to feature and promote women writers whenever possible.

ANA MARIA SPAGNA worked on backcountry trail crews for fifteen years in the North Cascades and wrote about her experiences in two essay collections: *Now Go Home* (2004), and *Potluck* (2011), both from Oregon State University Press. Her memoir/ history of the early civil rights movement, *Test Ride on the Sunnyland Bus* (Bison Books, 2010), won the *River Teeth* Literary Nonfiction Prize; she has twice been a finalist for the Washington State Book Award. Assistant Director of the Northwest Institute of Literary Arts' Whidbey Writers Workshop MFA program, she lives and writes in Stehekin, Washington, where she is also Chair of the Board of Commissioners for Chelan County Fire District #10. In 2012, she and her partner, Laurie Thompson, became the first same-sex couple to marry in rural Chelan County.

PATTI SULLIVAN has recently retired from a wide range of employment—fast food wait-staffing; department store display (which morphed into sales, retail management, and the "nightmare of customer service"); every office job to which temp agencies could send her (including bouts with obsolete addressograph and adding machines); and stints as an aerospace electronics plant technician, soldering under a microscope. She has two chapbooks, *For the Day* (DeerTree Press), and *Not Fade Away* (Finishing Line Press); poems and visual art in magazines; and in collaboration with her husband, poet Kevin Patrick Sullivan, artist books and exhibits at galleries, museums and display spaces. An organizer of the San Luis Obispo Poetry Festival and two reading series, Corners of the Mouth and Poetry at The Steynberg, she lives in San Luis Obispo.

MARIANNE SZLYK is an Associate Professor of English at Montgomery College and an associate poetry editor of the *Potomac Review*. Her poems have appeared in *Poppy Road Review*, *Poetry Pacific*, and *Storm Cycle 2013: The Best Kind of a Hurricane Press*. Book reviews have appeared in *Nineteenth-Century Gender Studies*, as well as essay-reviews on the work of Elizabeth Inchbald and Charlotte Smith. Szlyk's efforts on behalf of women involve teaching and mentoring, featuring women's books and perspectives in courses, and reviewing feminist literary studies for academic journals. In the 1990s, as an Administrative Secretary in the Athletics Department at MIT, Szlyk was involved in an unsuccessful effort to unionize clerical staff.

MARY ELLEN TALLEY grew up in Spokane and has worked as a speech-language pathologist in Washington state public schools since 1977. When her daughter was young, Mary Ellen was a Girl Scout co-leader; she has volunteered with her parish's women's shelter for twenty years. Her own mother returned to teaching when her youngest daughter entered first grade in 1956, to earn money for her daughters' college costs. Mary Ellen's poems have been published in *Redheaded Stepchild*, *Hospital Drive*, *Floating Bridge Pontoon* and *Main Street Rag*. She lives with her husband in Seattle. The poem included here is about her older sister who, in her mid-70s, still works part time.

LUCI TAPAHONSO (Navajo/Diné), originally from Shiprock, New Mexico, is the author of six books of poetry including *A Radiant Curve* (Arizona Book Award for Poetry, 2009). She has taught at the University of Kansas and the University of Arizona in Tucson, and is now professor of English Literature and Language at the University of New Mexico. In 2013, she was named the inaugural Poet Laureate of the Navajo Nation. Tapahonso has received Storyteller of the Year and Lifetime Achievement awards from the Native Writers Circle of the Americas; and a "Spirit of the Eagle" Leadership Award for her role in establishing the Indigenous Studies Program at the University of Kansas. Her work has appeared in many print and media productions in the US and internationally. Navajo was her first language, and she writes much of her poetry first in Diné Bizaad, then in English.

MARIA TERMINI, visual artist and poet, has been a carpenter and handyperson fixing up houses—work still dominated by men—because it was satisfying, paid well, and she was good at it. She says, "I didn't focus on not being as strong as a man. I found ways to direct my energy that let me do almost any job I took on," despite sometimes being accused of "taking jobs away from men." Termini says that "there is plenty of work for people who know what they are doing, no matter what their gender." She lives near Boston.

ELAINE TERRANOVA, born and raised in Philadelphia, educated at Temple University and the Vermont College MFA Program, has been a secretary, factory worker, salesgirl, pre-school teacher, and manuscript editor for Lippincott. For the past thirty-five years she has taught English and writing at Community College of Philadelphia, where many of her students are older women returning to school trying to better their prospects. Terranova also teaches for the MFA Program of Rutgers University, Camden. Her sixth and most recent book is *Dollhouse* (Off the Grid Press, 2013). Awards include a Pushcart Prize, an NEA grant, a Pew Fellowship, and the Walt Whitman Award for her first book, *The Cult of the Right Hand* (Doubleday).

GAIL TREMBLAY, of Onondaga/Mic Mac and French Canadian ancestry, is on the faculty at The Evergreen State College in Olympia, Washington, where she has mentored students since 1980 in visual arts, writing, and Native American and cultural studies. She shares her vision through multi-media visual works, installations, writing on Native American art, and poetry. Her books of poems include *Indian Singing* (Calyx Books, 1990); and *Farther From and Too Close to Home* (Lone Willow Press, 2014). Her poetry is widely anthologized and has been translated into French, German, Japanese, and Spanish. She is a past national president of the Woman's Caucus for Art, and active in the movement for women's equity in the arts.

NATASHA TRETHEWEY has four collections: *Domestic Work* (Cave Canem Poetry Prize, Graywolf Press, 2000), *Bellocq's Ophelia* (Graywolf, 2002), *Native Guard* (Houghton Mifflin, 2006, Pulitzer Prize 2007), and *Thrall* (Houghton Mifflin Harcourt, 2012); and a book of non-fiction, *Beyond Katrina: A Meditation on the Mississippi Gulf Coast* (University of Georgia Press, 2010). Born in Gulfport, Mississippi, to a white father and African American mother when mixed-raced marriages were still illegal in the South, Trethewey spent time in Atlanta and Gulfport (with her mother) and New Orleans (with her father) after her parents divorced. Her mother was murdered by her second husband, and Trethewey began writing to deal with her grief, encouraged by her father (poet Eric Trethewey). She was educated at the University of Georgia (BA), Hollins University (MA), and the University of Massachusetts (MFA); has taught at Auburn University, Duke and UNC-Chapel Hill, and since 2001 at Emory University in Atlanta. As U.S. Poet Laureate 2012-2014, she started a regular feature on the PBS NewsHour, "Where Poetry Lives."

STACEY K. VARGAS is a Professor of Physics at the Virginia Military Institute, researching the use of ultra-short pulsed lasers in wireless broadband telecommunications. She also has a laser spectroscopy research program that investigates the optical properties on ions doped into solid state crystals and glasses. She became a creative writer as a way to cope with encounters of gender discrimination and sexual harassment in her career as a female physicist. She hopes her voice will encourage others to use theirs.

DAVI WALDERS has had poetry and prose appear in more than two hundred anthologies and journals. Her collections include *Women against Tyranny: Poems of Resistance during the Holocaust* (Clemson University Digital Press, 2011) and *Using Poetry in Therapeutic Settings* (Vital Signs Poetry Project). She developed the Vital Signs Project at NIH in Bethesda, Maryland, which was funded by The Witter Bynner Foundation and for which she received Hadassah of Greater Washington's Myrtle Wreath Award. Other awards include a Maryland Artist Grant in Poetry, an Alden B. Dow Creativity Fellowship, and fellowships at the VCCA and Hebrew Union College in Cincinnati. Her work has been read on the Writer's Almanac, nominated for Pushcart Prizes, and choreographed and performed in New York, Cleveland, and elsewhere.

SHANNON CAMLIN WARD is author of the chapbook, *Blood Creek* (Longleaf Press, 2013), and a winner of the 2013 Nazim Hikmet Poetry Prize. She has received residencies at Yaddo, Norton Island, and the Anderson Center. Her poems have appeared in *Great River Review, Superstition Review, and Tar River Poetry*. Under the direction of Dorianne Laux, she received an MFA from North Carolina State University in 2009. She lives with her spouse in Fayetteville, North Carolina, and teaches composition at her alma mater, Methodist University. In 2013, she volunteered as a mentor with the Afghan Women's Writing Project.

BELLE WARING (1951 - 2015) is the author of *Refuge* (University of Pittsburgh Press, 1990), which won the AWP Award in 1989, the Washington Prize in 1991, and was cited by *Publishers Weekly* as one of the best books of 1990; and *Dark Blonde* (Sarabande Books, 1997), which won the San Francisco Poetry Center Prize and the Larry Levis Reading Prize in 1998. Waring worked as a neo-natal intensive care nurse, as Writer-in-Residence at Children's National Medical Center in Washington D.C., and as a librarian and science writer at the National Institute of Health. She passed away in early 2015.

SARAH BROWN WEITZMAN has published in numerous journals, such as *America*, *Earth's Daughters*, *North American Review*, *Rattle*, *Mid-American Review*, *Poet Lore*, *Potomac Review*, and *U.S. Catholic*. In the 1970s, she was an early member of the Feminist Writers' Union, and contributed articles to their newsletter. A Pushcart nominee, she received a Fellowship from the NEA in 1984. Her latest book is a children's novel, *Herman and the Ice Witch*, published by Main Street Rag. She lives in southern coastal Florida.

KAREN J. WEYANT is the author of two chapbooks, *Stealing Dust* (Finishing Line Press, 2009) and *Wearing Heels in the Rust Belt* (Main Street Rag, 2012); her work has appeared in many journals and newspapers. She teaches at Jamestown Community College in Jamestown, New York, where the majority of her students have working-class backgrounds. Before she became a poet and professor, she worked a variety of blue collar jobs including a brief stint as a third-shift factory worker. She now lives and writes in the Rust Belt of northern Pennsylvania.

LAURA MADELINE WISEMAN is the author of more than a dozen books and chapbooks and the editor of *Women Write Resistance: Poets Resist Gender Violence* (Hyacinth Girl Press, 2013). She has volunteered and taught poetry workshops in crisis shelters for women, and book sales from *Women Write Resistance* readings have been donated to organizations that support women. Recent books are *American Galactic* (Martian Lit Books, 2014), *Some Fatal Effects of Curiosity and Disobedience* (Lavender Ink, 2014), and *Queen of the Platform* (Anaphora Literary Press, 2013). She holds a doctorate from the University of Nebraska, has received an Academy of American Poets Award, a Mari Sandoz/*Prairie Schooner* Award, and the Wurlitzer Foundation Fellowship.

DEBORAH WOODARD is the author of six books of poetry and translation, most recently *Borrowed Tales* (Stockport Flats, 2012). Her translation from the Italian of Amelia Rosselli's *Hospital Series* is forthcoming from New Directions. She is currently working on a new collection, *From Us to All of You*, about her mother's life in Vermont in the fifties, including her labor and Socialist affiliations. Deborah teaches hybrid literature and creative writing classes at the Richard Hugo House, a community literary center in Seattle. Born in New York, raised in Vermont, with an MFA in Poetry from UC Irvine, Deborah completed a PhD in English from the University of Washington, where she wrote her dissertation on early Modernist women poets.

SUSAN YUZNA holds a BA in English from the University of Iowa and a MFA from the University of Montana, where she was the Richard Hugo Poetry Scholar. Her books are *Her Slender Dress* (1996), winner of the Akron Poetry Prize and the Norma Farber First Book Award; and *Pale Bird, Spouting Fire* (2000), both from the University of Akron Press. She has held a Bush Artist Fellowship and a Minnesota State Arts Board Grant, and residencies at Yaddo, MacDowell, Djerassi, and Ucross. In her writing, Yuzna looks at traditions of women struggling for fulfillment—she has helped incarcerated women with correspondence, and is exploring this hidden world through poetry. She has taught at many colleges and universities, and lives in Minneapolis.

Born and raised in Detroit, **SARAH ZALE** lives in Port Townsend, Washington, and teaches writing and social justice in Seattle. She is founder and director of the Listening Tree Project, a program that raises awareness of privilege, power, and oppression, and promotes activism related to gender, sexual orientation, race, age, and physical ability. Her recent collection, *Sometimes You Do Things* (Aquarius Press, 2013), highlights Detroit's history and celebrates its rebuilding. Naomi Shihab Nye chose a poem of hers as a finalist in the 2011 Split This Rock Poetry Contest.

ANDRENA ZAWINSKI, daughter and granddaughter of steel mill laborers and coal miners, was born and raised in Pittsburgh, Pennsylvania, and has made Alameda, California her home. Her poetry collections include *Traveling in Reflected Light* (Pig Iron Press), which won a Kenneth Patchen prize; and *Something About* (Blue Light Press), which received a PEN Oakland Josephine Miles Award. She also has four chapbooks, with poems appearing widely online and in print. She founded the San Francisco Bay Area Women's Poetry Salon and is editor of their anthology, *Turning a Train of Thought Upside Down* (Scarlet Tanager Press). *PoetryMagazine.com's* Features Editor since 2000, Zawinski has made fish lures, waited tables, filed legal briefs, and worked as a feminist organizer, but has been a writer and educator most of her life.

LEAH ZAZULYER'S awareness of women's issues was inspired by her mother, who emigrated alone at fifteen to Chicago, went immediately to work in sweatshops of the garment industry, and soon became a founding member of the International Ladies' Garment Worker's Union. In recent years, Leah has been involved in the Eastman School of Music's "Women's Music and Poetry Festival." As a translator of Yiddish poetry and a poet herself, she has been privileged to help promote increasing attention being paid to the writing of women. As a former special education teacher, school psychologist, consultant, and play therapist, she has often focused on the needs of female students.

PERMISSIONS AND PUBLICATION CREDITS

Kim Addonizio, from *Jimmy & Rita* (BOA Editions 1997; reissued 2013 by Stephen Austin State University Press). Copyright © by Kim Addonizio. Reprinted by permission of the author.

Mary Alexandra Agner, "Ordinary Women Scientists." Used by permission of the author.

Dorothy Alexander, "Honest Work," from *The Art of Digression: Scraps, Orts & Fragments* (Village Books, 2014). Copyright by Dorothy Alexander. Used by permission.

Kathya Alexander, "Naa Naa." Used by permission of the author.

Takako Arai, "When the Moon Rises," from *Soul Dance: Poems by Takako Arai*, translated by Jeffrey Angles (Mi'Te Press, 2008). Used by permission of author and translator.

Wendy Barker, "Ending the Semester in Am Lit," from *The Southern Review*. Copyright © 2014. Reprinted by permission of the author.

Ellen Bass, "Phone Therapy," from *Mules of Love*. Copyright © 2002 by Ellen Bass. Reprinted with the permission of The Permissions Company, Inc., on behalf of BOA Editions Ltd., www.boaeditions.org.

Grace Bauer, "Modern Clothing," from *Retreats & Recognitions* (Lost Horse Press, 2007). Copyright © 2007 by Grace Bauer. Reprinted by permission of the author.

Sandra Beasley, "Vocation," from *I Was the Jukebox: Poems*. Copyright © 2010 by Sandra Beasley. Used with permission of W.W. Norton & Company.

Jan Beatty, from *The Switching/Yard* (University of Pittsburgh Press, 2013). Reprinted by permission of the author.

Shaindel Beers, from *A Brief History of Time* (Salt Publishing, 2009). First published in *Hunger Mountain*, #8, Spring 2006. Copyright © 2009 by Shaindel Beers. Reprinted by permission of the author.

Lytton Bell, "Another Day at the Dildo Factory," from *Poetica Erotica*, Volume I, 2012. First published in *Exquisite Corpse*, www.corpse.org, December 2001. Reprinted by permission of the author.

Rosebud Ben-Oni, "At Ten I Held the Look of Locust," first appeared in *SOLECISM* (Virtual Artists' Collective, 2013). Reprinted by permission of the author.

Judith Ayn Bernhard, "Adolfo or Rodolfo?" from *Prisoners of Culture* (CC Marimbo, Berkeley, 2014). Copyright © 2014 by Judith Ayn Bernhard. Reprinted by permission of the author.

Sheila Black, "My Mission is to Surprise and Delight," from Split this Rock Blogspot, Poem of the Week, 21 February 2014: http://blogthisrock.blogspot.com/2014/02/poem-of-week-sheila-black.html

Barbara Drake, "The Typist" from *Windfall*, Spring 2011 (as part of an editorial discussing poetry about work). Used by permission of the author.

Patricia Dubrava, "The End of Offices (1)." Used by permission of the author.

Denise Duhamel, "Unemployment," from the poem sequence entitled "Recession Commandments," from *Blowout*. Copyright © 2013 by Denise Duhamel. Reprinted by permission of the University of Pittsburgh Press.

Camille T. Dungy, "7 Problems in Pedagogy," from *Solo Café 8 & 9: Teachers & Students*, Vol. 2 (2013), ed. Lenard D. Moore. Used by permission of the author.

Susan Eisenberg, "Partner #3," from *Pioneering: Poems from the Construction Site* (ILR/Cornell University Press, 1998). First published in *Prairie Schooner*. Reprinted by permission of the author.

Jennifer Fandel, "A Powerful Poem," from *The Chiron Review* (Issue 83, Winter 2009). Reprinted by permission of the author.

Nikky Finney, "Labor Strike," from *The World is Round: Poems*. Copyright © 2013 by Nikky Finney. First edition Copyright © by Lynn Carol Nikky Finney. First published in the United States by InnerLight Publishing, 2003. This edition published in 2013 by Triquarterly Books/ Northwestern University Press by arrangement with Nikky Finney. All rights reserved.

Kathleen Flenniken, "Siren Recognition," from *Plume* (University of Washington Press, 2012). Copyright © 2012 by the University of Washington Press. Used by permission.

Stefanie Freele, from *Surrounded by Water* (Press 53, 2012). First published in *Mid-American Review*, Vol. XXXII, Nos. 1 & 2, Fall 2011-Spring 2012. Copyright © 2012 by Stefanie Freele. Reprinted by permission of the author.

Sarah Freligh, "Waitress" from the chapbook, *A Brief Natural History of An American Girl* (Accents Publishing, 2012). Used by permission of the author.

Daisy Fried, "Little Girls Weaving," from *She Didn't Mean to Do It* (University of Pittsburgh Press, 2001). Copyright © 2001 by Daisy Fried. Used by permission of the University of Pittsburgh Press.

Erin Fristad, "Advice to Female Deckhands," from *New Poets of the American West*, ed. Lowell Jaegar (Many Voices Press, 2010). Also published in *Working the Woods, Working the Sea: An Anthology of Northwest Writings*, ed. Finn Wilcox & Jerry Gorsline (Empty Bowl, 2008). First published in *Stringtown #8*, 2005.

Maria Mazziotti Gillan, "At the Factory Where My Mother Worked." An earlier version of this poem, "The Cigar Factories in Yuba City, Florida," appeared in *Ancestors' Song* (Bordighera Press, 2013). Reprinted by permission of the author.

Diana García, from *When Living Was a Labor Camp* (University of Arizona Press, 2000). First published in *Ploughshares*, Vol. 22, No. 1, Spring 1996. Reprinted by permission of the author.

Cindy Williams Gutiérrez, from *the small claim of bones* (Bilingual Press/*Editorial Bilingüe*, 2014). Reprinted by permission of the author and publisher.

Stephanie Barbé Hammer, "Memo to the Factory of Tears (for Valzhyna Mort)," from *How Formal?* (Spout Hill Press, 2014). Copright © 2014 by Stephanie Barbé Hammer. Reprinted by permission of the author.

Janice N. Harrington, "Pietà," from *The Hands of Strangers: Poems from the Nursing Home.* Copyright © 2011 by Janice N. Harrington. Reprinted with the permission of The Permissions Company, Inc., on behalf of BOA Editions, Ltd., www.boaeditions.org.

Jana Harris, from *The Dust of Everyday Life: an Epic Poem of the Pacific Northwest* (Sasquatch Books, 1997). Copyright © 1997 by Jana Harris. Reprinted by permission of the author.

Sharon Hashimoto, "Four Weeks Unemployed, I Fail the Water Department's Lift and Carry Exam," from *The Crane Wife* (Story Line Press, 2003). First published in the *Carolina Quarterly*, Fall 1990. Used by permission of the author.

Linda M. Hasselstrom, "Clara: In the Post Office," from *Roadkill* (Spoon River Poetry Press, 1987); and *Dakota Bones: Collected Poems of Linda M. Hasselstrom* (Spoon River, 1993). Copyright © 1997 & 1993, Spoon River Publishing. Reprinted with permission.

Linda Hogan, "Woman Chopping Wood," from *Dark. Sweet.: New & Selected Poems* (Coffee House Press, 2014). Copyright © 2014 by Linda Hogan. Reprinted by permission of Coffee House Press.

Cathy Park Hong, "Engines Within the Throne," from *Engine Empire: Poems.* Copyright © 2012 by Cathy Park Hong. Reprinted with permission of W.W. Norton. All rights reserved.

Carolina Hospital, "Mourning Doves." Used by permission of the author.

Holly J. Hughes, "Working on Deck," from *Boxing the Compass* (Floating Bridge Press, 2007), and *Sailing by Ravens* (University of Alaska Press, 2014). First appeared in *Pontoon 6* and *The Hedgebrook Journal 2000.* Copyright by Holly J. Hughes. Reprinted by permission of the author.

Luisa A. Igloria, from *Juan Luna's Revolver* (University of Notre Dame Press, 2009). Reprinted by permission of the author.

Arlitia Jones, "Shit Job," from *The Bandsaw Riots* (Bear Star Press, 2001). First published in *Hayden's Ferry Review*, #28, Spring/Summer 2001. Reprinted by permission of the author.

Vandana Khanna, "Earning America," from *Afternoon Masala* (University of Arkansas Press, 2014). Previously published as "Working" in the *Indiana Review.* Reprinted by permission of the author.

Carolyn Kizer, "Union of Women," from *Cool, Calm & Collected: Poems 1960-2000* (Copper Canyon Press, 2001). First published in *The Progressive.* Reprinted with the permission of The Permissions Company, Inc., on behalf of Copper Canyon Press, www.coppercanyonpress.org.

Melissa Kwasny, "Industry," from *The Petroleum Manga*, by Marina Zurkow, edited by Valerie Vogrin (Peanut Books, an imprint of punctum books, 2013). Used by permission of the author.

231

Poems (Firebrand Books, 1993); and the anthology *Coffee Break Secrets* (Word of Mouth Productions, 1988). Used by permission of the author.

Rikki Santer, "RE: Secretaries from Hell," from *Earth Daughters* #74 ("Soapbox" issue). Reprinted by permission of the author.

Penelope Scambly Schott, "'*And how are you gentlemen on this fine fall evening?*'" from *Lillie Was a Goddess, Lillie Was a Whore* (Mayapple Press, 2013). Copyright © 2013 by Penelope Scambly Schott. Used by permission of the author.

Willa Schneberg, "Into the Social Worker's Office Walks Vietnam's Legacy" (as "Into My Office Walks Vietnam's Legacy"), from *Storytelling in Cambodia* (Calyx Books, 2006). Reprinted by permission of the author.

Elaine Sexton, "Class," from *Causeway.* Copyright © 2008 by Elaine Sexton. Used with permission of *New Issues Poetry & Prose,* Western Michigan University.

Laura Shovan, "The Mammographer." Used by permission of the author.

Sandy Shreve, from *The Speed of the Wheel Is Up to the Potter* (Kingston, Ontario: Quarry Press, 1990). Reprinted with permission of the author.

Martha Silano, "Pale Blue Dot," from *Reckless Lovely* (Saturnalia Books, 2014). Previously published in *North American Review,* Vol. 298, No. 4, Fall 2013. Reprinted by permission of Saturnalia Books and the author.

Ana Maria Spagna, "The Only Girl on the Trail Crew." Used by permission of the author.

Patti Sullivan, "Dog Eat Dog." Used by permission of the author.

Marianne Szlyk, "A Paralegal in DC," from *Listening to Electric Cambodia, Looking at Trees of Heaven* (Kind of a Hurricane Press). First published in *The Linden Avenue Literary Journal* (#4, 2012). Reprinted by permission of the author.

Mary Ellen Talley, "Ghazal: Unbuckled Shoes." Used by permission of the author.

Luci Tapahonso, "Hard to Take," from *Seasonal Woman* (Tooth of Time Books, 1982). Copyright © 1982 by Luci Tapahonso. Reprinted by permission of the author.

Maria Termini, "Chandelier." Used by permission of the author.

Elaine Terranova, "In the Bindery," from *Damages* (Copper Canyon Press, 1995). First published in *Slipstream.* Reprinted by permission of the author.

Eugenia Toledo, "Stories of Women." First published in *New Letters,* Vol. 76, No. 4, Fall 2010. Reprinted by permission of the author and Carolyne Wright (translator).

ABOUT THE EDITORS

M.L. LYONS was born and raised in Southern California. She has worked as a publicist and screenwriter in the entertainment industry, a college instructor, a marketing communications writer for IT firms, and an editor and grant-writer for literary arts organizations in the Northwest. Lyons was awarded a Klepser Fellowship and earned an MFA in Creative Writing at the University of Washington. She translated the poetry of Forough Farrokhzad as part of her MFA thesis on Farrokhzad's influence on modern Persian poetry. A longtime advocate for women's rights, she created the first Women in the Arts Festival at the University of Washington. Her poetry and prose have appeared in *Raven Chronicles, Terrain.org* and *Pontoon*, among other publications. She lives near Seattle.

EUGENIA TOLEDO was born in Temuco, Chile, grew up in the same neighborhood as Pablo Neruda, completed higher degrees in Spanish, and came to the U.S. for doctoral studies after her university instructorship was terminated following the 1973 military coup. She received an M.A. in Latin American Literature and a Ph.D. in Spanish Literature from the University of Washington, and settled in Seattle to teach and write. She has published four collections of poetry in Spanish and a text entitled *Creative Writing* (forthcoming in 2015). An award-winning bilingual manuscript of poems is *Trazas de mapa, trazas de sangre / Map Traces, Blood Traces*—written after a return visit to Chile in 2008 with Carolyne Wright. Poems of hers in translation by Wright have appeared widely. With her husband, Toledo divides her time between Temuco and Seattle.

CAROLYNE WRIGHT is the author of nine books of poetry, four volumes of poetry in translation from Spanish and Bengali; and a collection of essays. She lived in Chile on a Fulbright Grant during the presidency of Salvador Allende, and spent four years on fellowships in India and Bangladesh, translating Bengali women poets. After visiting positions at universities around the country, Wright returned to her native Seattle in 2005, and teaches for the Northwest Institute of Literary Arts' MFA Program and for Seattle's Richard Hugo House. A Contributing Editor for the Pushcart Prizes and a Senior Editor for Lost Horse Press, she has also been a waitress, hotel maid, hospital clerk, freelance proofreader and textbook developmental editor, substitute bilingual 4th grade teacher, and Latin America sales liaison for a biotech firm (requiring fluency in Spanish and Portuguese).